DISCARD

S0-BEJ-139

NOBODY MEETS BIGFOOT

NOBODY MEETS BIGFOOT

• • •

Marian T. Place

DODD, MEAD & COMPANY
NEW YORK

Wm. Walker Library
School District No. 48

Copyright © 1976 by Marian T. Place
All rights reserved
No part of this book may be reproduced in any form
without permission in writing from the publisher
Printed in the United States of America
by The Cornwall Press, Inc., Cornwall, N.Y.

Library of Congress Cataloging in Publication Data

Place, Marian Templeton.
  Nobody meets Bigfoot.

  SUMMARY: A young boy accompanies his adventurous
grandmother on an expedition searching for Bigfoot in
the Northwest forests.
  [1. Sasquatch—Fiction] I. Title.
PZ7.P69No   [Fic]   75–40030
ISBN 0–396–07290–9

Contents

You may have heard the story, too
Of how upon Mount Siskiyou
Was seen an ape, or spook, or tramp,
In region near to Happy Camp . . .

That was of stature taller than
The ordinary height of man—
Who fed on berries, roots and brouse,
Nor, of abode, had tent or house . . .

And from whose eye
There gleamed the fierceness of the beast
That, thwarted of voracious feast,
With sullenness, feigns to retire
Far in the jungle, to his lair . . .

from "The Hermit of Siskiyou"
by L. W. Musick
Crescent City, California, 1896

1

• • •

The Number Five Nobody

When Bud Miller entered the kitchen for breakfast, his mother was cooking sausages and hotcakes. He padded barefooted across the linoleum and sniffed hungrily over her shoulder. She gave him an affectionate peck on the ear. "Morning, dear. Hotcakes coming up in a minute."

Bud popped a sausage into his mouth and joined the rest of the family at the table. "Morning, everybody."

"Morning," his father, older brother, and older sister answered from behind pages of the morning newspaper. No one bothered to look at him, or ask him how he felt. To attract their attention, he gulped his orange juice noisily. When no one made a comment, he began tapping his knife against the glass. When that went unnoticed, Bud talked to himself. He often carried on conversations with himself when the family ignored him, or he was by himself, which amounted to the same thing.

"I sure like Saturday mornings," he told himself. For one thing he could sleep in as long as he wanted. Actually, on Saturday mornings the entire family, including the cat and dog, slept in an extra hour or two. No alarms jangled, the dog didn't bark, the telephone was silent, and his older sister was forbidden to switch on her stereo full volume the moment she wakened.

Another reason he liked Saturday mornings was because everybody appeared at the table in a relaxed mood. They behaved almost like those families viewed on television commercials. His father didn't gulp his coffee and rush off to work. His mother didn't put on her wig with one hand, prepare breakfast with the other, and dash off to the school where she taught. She didn't send Bud back upstairs to put on a clean shirt, either. And Larry or Pam didn't nag him about spilling milk on the table instead of in his cereal bowl. He could come to the table in his pajamas, with his brown hair uncombed, and no one said he looked like Beau, their sheep dog.

But best of all, Bud reminded himself, he liked Saturday mornings because his mother made hotcakes. He could eat a dozen and float them in syrup, and no one picked on him about *that*. He could eat with his elbows on the table, too. If he felt like it, he could cook his own hotcakes. Some Saturday mornings he was in the mood for hotcakes the size of silver dollars. Afterwards he could brag to his pals, "I ate forty-two hotcakes," and be telling the truth, cross-his-heart or hope-to-you-know-what. Or, he might feel like saucer-sized hotcakes, or dinner plate-sized ones. They were very tricky to turn without splattering dough all over the stove.

Once he experimented with making a super-giant-sized hotcake which filled the skillet. When it looked ready to turn, he slipped a spatula under the right half, another spatula under the left half, and counted to three before he flipped. Either his timing was off, or the batter wasn't cooked enough on the under-side. Most of it flipped on his pajama top, and dribbled down his legs and bare feet onto the linoleum. While he hopped around, yowling because the batter scorched his toes, his father roared that it was a crime to waste good food in such dingbat foolishness. His mother ordered him to clean up the mess. His brother and sister made smart-aleck remarks. Only the dog helped by licking up the blobs on the floor. No one sympathized with Bud, or handed him the burn ointment, or said, "Good try, ol' chap. Better luck next time." But then, that was what a

11

fellow had to expect when he was the Number Five Nobody in the Miller family.

Being the youngest in the family made him the Number Five Nobody. No matter what came up for a family vote . . . shall we go to a ballgame or a concert, do we have spaghetti or hamburgers, do we watch the late-late horror movie or go to bed . . . Bud was outvoted. The only time he got to choose first, and have the family agree with his choice, was when he chose to do something all the others planned to do anyway. Being the Number Five Nobody in a family made a fellow an expert on minority rights, discrimination, third-class citizenship, unequal representation, unequal allowances, and other deadly forms of family nobody-itis.

Fortunately this morning, before Bud got a running start on feeling sorry for himself, his mother placed two platters on the table, and sat down. By the time the others folded their newspapers, Bud had filled his plate and had first grab on the syrup pitcher.

"Good breakfast," everybody complimented Mrs. Miller.

No one said anything more until the platters were empty. Then Mrs. Miller poured herself and her husband a second cup of coffee, and glanced at the bulletin board on the wall. Since this was the first day of summer vacation, she sighed happily. "Do

12

you realize there is not one single thing we have to do today? We can all relax!"

However, before anyone could cheer, the doorbell rang. The family blinked at one another. They weren't used to having the doorbell ring on Saturday mornings.

"Oh, it's probably the paper boy," Mrs. Miller guessed.

"He collects on Monday nights," Pam reminded her.

When the doorbell rang again, Mr. Miller said, "Will somebody please answer the door?"

Pam pretended she didn't hear, so Larry ordered Bud, "Get movin'."

So Bud did. What else could the Number Five Nobody do? He returned shortly with a letter. "It's a special delivery from Grammy Miller." He handed it to his father and slid back into his chair.

Mr. Miller chuckled. "I'm almost afraid to open it. You know your grandmother. The only time she writes is when she's leaving on some crazy expedition, and it's too late to stop her."

Pam and Larry giggled, but not Bud. "Why do you say that? Gram doesn't get into trouble."

Pam informed him that their father worried because Grammy wasn't the kind of old lady who wore white gloves and went to old lady-type parties.

Larry rolled his eyes. "Right! Even women my

age don't traipse off to the Aleutian Islands to trap sea otter. Or explore caves. Or hunt for dinosaur bones."

"What's wrong with doing what you want to do?" Bud demanded. Suddenly he felt a warm kinship for his grandmother because she did the sort of things he would do, if he had the chance.

"Well, we'll soon know what she's up to," his father said, opening the letter. He began reading aloud: *"Dear Family. My, how time flies. Here it is summer and I still haven't used those pretty hankies you sent me at Christmas. I did thank you for them, didn't I? I hope you're all fine, and looking forward to a fine summer vacation. I surely am. The most exciting thing has happened."* Here Mr. Miller paused, and groaned softly. *"A biology teacher from a college nearby has organized a small expedition to search the mountains of northern California for a giant hairy apelike monster repeatedly seen there by loggers and hikers."*

"Monster!" Bud gasped, almost choking on the word.

"Monster!" the others exclaimed.

His father resumed reading: *"Some people call this monster an Abominable Snowman, but that's silly. Northern California doesn't have as much snow as the Himalayan Mountains. Anyway, this monster has been seen frequently, and the teacher told me some man had taken a picture of it. Imagine that!*

14

When I called the teacher and asked if I might join his group, he said I was welcome. I said I wasn't exactly young. He just laughed and said to come anyway. So, for the past week I have been shopping. It's hard to know what to take on a monster hunt."

"She's serious!" Pam said. "Mom, where in the world would Grammy be going? A monster couldn't hide on Lassen Peak or Mount Shasta, could it? I mean, didn't we see those peaks from the highway the time we drove north from Disneyland to Portland?"

Without being aware of it, Mrs. Miller lapsed into her classroom voice. She declared there still were extremely remote primitive mountainous areas in northwestern California. Also, she did recall reading something about a monster which people called Bigfoot, or Sasquatch, or something. "But, Ed, the mountains of northwestern California are very rugged. You really should put your foot down, and tell your mother she simply must not go on such a wild goose chase."

"Not goose chase. Monster chase," Bud said, chortling. Then he demanded to know what was so awful about a monster hunt. "I think it sounds great. You're acting as if Grammy was going by herself, but she isn't. She's going on an expedition."

Edith Miller relaxed. "Bud is right. Read the rest of the letter, dear."

Bud was right. His grandmother made it very

clear in her letter that the group would look after her. *"I shall be perfectly comfortable in my Wigwam."*

"Wigwam!" Bud shouted.

"Grammy's going to stay with Indians?" Pam added.

"What's wrong with that?" Bud bristled. "I'd sleep in a wigwam if I had the chance." A couple of years before when the family visited the Idaho State Fair, Bud had spent fifty cents of his allowance to sit inside a real wigwam, and hear an Indian describe how his people lived before the white men came.

Mr. Miller reminded Bud to stop interrupting. He continued reading: *"It's a shame one of the children can't keep me company. But I wouldn't think of interfering with their summer activities or the family vacation. But if one of them can join me, let me know right away. There are good plane connections between Boise and Portland, Oregon. Since I want to drive up to Portland to see some friends, I could meet Larry or Pam or Bud there. But if no one can come, I will understand. Wish me luck. Maybe I will get to shake hands with the hairy ape-man. Love to all, Mother."*

Everyone was silent until finally Mr. Miller said, "One of us ought to go with her. But I just can't. My vacation is scheduled for August. Edith, you've signed up for summer school. What about you, Larry?"

Larry slumped in his chair. "Golly, Dad, what would my boss say if I asked for time off from sacking groceries to help my grandmother search for a monster? And jobs are too hard to find. I don't want to chance losing mine."

Pam assured her father hastily that she would love to go, only she had to see the orthodontist every week.

All four looked at Bud.

Bud was quivering with excitement. "You mean, I can go?" He had held his breath for fear his father or mother or brother or sister would be the lucky one. "Wow, wow, wow!" Of course, it would mean missing out on the chance to beat Doug at qualifying for the swim team, or racking up more miles on his bike than Doug or Ronnie, his next-to-best friend. They were always beating him at something. But if he went on a genuine monster hunt, they'd turn greener than school lunch pea soup. Nothing they would do all summer could top a monster hunt.

His father beamed at him. "You'll be a great help to your grandmother, especially since you passed that course on how to survive in the wilderness."

"It's the chance of a lifetime," Larry assured him.

"Yeah," Bud murmured softly. It sure beat sacking groceries or going to the dentist.

"Tell you what," his father added. "You really are doing the family a favor, and Grammy, too. If you go, I'll buy you that transistorized tape recorder you've been pestering for."

"Sure I'll go!" Bud rolled his eyes and hugged himself. "How soon can I leave?"

His father glanced at the clock on the kitchen wall. "Why don't I call Grammy right now? The sooner things are settled, the better for everyone."

2

• • •

A Wigwam with Hot and Cold Running Water

Early the following Thursday morning the Miller family accompanied Bud to the airport at Boise, Idaho. After his ticket was stamped and his baggage placed on a cart, his mother not only paper-clipped his ticket and boarding pass to his shirt pocket, she marched him onto the plane, seated him and snapped his seat belt. Moments after she left, the plane took off on its smooth flight to Portland.

Grammy Miller was at the gate to greet him. She was the kind who could kiss a grandson without smearing lipstick on his nose. She assured Bud she was thrilled to see him. Every year he looked more and more like Grampy Miller. "My, you're so tall for your age! You're almost a grown man." Thank goodness! She needed a man's help because the monster hunt would take place in a primitive area high in the mountains. She would feel much safer having an experienced mountaineer looking after her.

The compliments made Bud feel six feet tall. Still, he replied modestly, "Aw, I'm not that great. You sure look good, Grammy." Except for her short white curly hair and a few wrinkles, his grandmother appeared quite youthful. She was slim, deeply tanned, and clad in faded blue jeans, a plaid shirt, and tennis shoes. "Hey, you're still wearing Grampy's watch."

Grammy patted the large old-fashioned wristwatch encased in a worn leather wristband. "I'd be lost without it. Well! Let's not stand out here. What say we head for the mountains?"

"We have to claim my baggage." Bud handed her the tickets and check stubs, assuming she would do everything for him as his mother did.

Grammy gave them back. "That's your job. Grampy always looked after our baggage."

"I don't know how to claim my baggage."

Grammy told him to read the signs and follow the arrows. "Pretend you're following clues in a treasure hunt. I'll hop along to the parking lot and meet you out in front of the terminal." She waved off.

Bud was thunderstruck. His mother would be horrified if she knew he'd been left alone to find his way through a strange, large air terminal. Grammy must think he had sense enough to handle the job without explaining every little step, the way his mother did. He'd show Grammy she was right. He strode into the terminal, spied a sign saying BAGGAGE, and followed lighted flashing arrows to an area where there were three large revolving carrousels. He watched luggage move down long chutes onto the carrousels. Passengers lifted their suitcases off and carried them to a checkstand. A clerk compared the stubs on the luggage with those in the travelers' hands. If the numbers matched, the clerk permitted the passengers to move on through an electrically controlled glass door to the outside of the terminal.

For a moment Bud was frightened. The baggage claim area was crowded and noisy. He didn't know which carrousel to approach. But he rapped his knuckles on his head three times and told himself, "Use the ol' bean, Miller." After studying a bit he noticed flight numbers posted above each carrousel, and recognized 28 as his. "Smart guy, Miller," he congratulated himself. In less than five minutes he was outside the building, duffel bag in one hand, sleeping bag in the other. Whew!

"Over here," his grandmother called from a parking slot. She stood at the rear of a red pickup truck which had a white camper unit mounted on the truck bed. After she tossed Bud's belongings inside the camper and locked the door, she and Bud took their places in the truck cab. As they buckled their safety belts Grammy cautioned, "We're not going to be able to talk for a time. The traffic will be very fast and nerve-racking. I'll need to concentrate on my driving."

Bud understood. Fortunately traffic moved slowly out of the airport, so Grammy had no problem locating the on-ramp to the southbound I-5 freeway. But once the rig merged with the swift six-lane traffic, Bud started biting his fingernails. Trucks, buses, and cars roared past them to the left and right, often changing lanes so suddenly that Bud shouted, "Look out, Grammy!" She maneuvered into the far-right slow lane and finally glanced briefly at Bud. "Kind of wild, wasn't it?"

"Wow, wow, wow!" Bud agreed. "You're a better driver than Dad. You don't swear and change lanes the way he does."

Grammy chuckled. "This old pickup is like its driver, pokey but dependable."

"Can we talk now?" When his grandmother nodded, Bud asked how long it would take them to get where they were going, wherever that was.

He learned that the headquarters for the monster hunt would be on upper Bluff Creek in northwestern California, some five hundred miles away. After they crossed the Siskiyou Mountains on the Oregon-California boundary, they would camp overnight beside the Klamath River. Tomorrow they would follow the river canyon downstream a hundred miles into the mountains. By lunchtime they should reach another campground at the confluence of Bluff Creek and the Klamath River, and meet their new friends.

Bud's next question was, "When did you buy the new camper for the pickup?"

"A week ago." She hated to give up the old one in which she had shared many hours with Grampy. "But now that he's gone and the old camper was really worn out, I didn't feel so badly about trading it in for a new model. It's so fancy! It has a stove and refrigerator, and a bathroom, and hot and cold running water."

Bud wondered aloud if they would sleep in it after they reached the Indian village.

"What Indian village?"

"You wrote you would be staying in a wigwam."

His grandmother laughed. "Oh, dear. I didn't mean we would sleep in a real wigwam. This camper model is called a Wigwam. That's the manufacturer's brand name."

Bud's jaw sagged, and then he burst out laughing. "You sure fooled me! Wait till I tell Doug." Suddenly he smote his forehead and moaned, "Oh—no!"

"Trouble?" Grammy inquired.

Big trouble, Bud confessed, blushing. "Doug's my best friend. I really laid it on to him about sleeping in a wigwam, a *chief's* wigwam. Yech! Wait till I tell him I slept in a wigwam with hot and cold running water. He'll laugh me off the planet." Bud slouched against his seat belt, murmuring sadly, "Wow, wow, wow." When his grandmother didn't sympathize with him, he complained, "Gee, at least you could say you feel sorry for me."

Grammy asked for one good reason why she should. "Now, if you were a baby and had skinned your knee—"

"I'm not a baby!"

Grammy patted his shoulder. "Then stop making a mountain out of a can of beans."

Bud's face cleared, and he grinned. "Mole hill," he corrected her.

"Mole hill? What mole hill?"

"It's not 'Stop making a mountain out of a can of beans.' It's 'Stop making a mountain out of a mole hill.' "

Grammy pursed her lips. "I like beans better."

"Mole hill!"

"Beans!"

The two laughed, and rode on happily until Bud groaned. "Hey, you weren't kidding about the monster hunt, were you?"

Grammy tried hard not to smile. "You told Doug about that, too?"

Bud nodded slowly. "Yeah. I r-e-ally laid it on. Doug believed me, but Ronnie said you had to be kidding. Ronnie's my next-to-best friend. He said there weren't any giant hairy apes in North America, except in zoos. I said there were *too* huge hairy monsters in northern California or you wouldn't be going there on a monster hunt. Doug backed me up. He said he saw a movie about a real live monster nicknamed Bigfoot. It was seven feet tall, and hairy all over, and left footprints twenty-two inches long."

Grammy's eyes sparkled. "Bigfoot is the monster we're going to hunt! I saw the movie Doug mentioned, and that television special on monsters. Did you?"

"No, and Ronnie said that movie was a fake. The monster was only a man wearing a monkey suit. Dick—he's Ronnie's best friend—said he read a library book about a monster called Sasquatch. It kidnapped this guy, and hauled him off to a secret valley where the monster's family lived. The guy escaped before they ate him for breakfast, so that's how come he lived to write about his adventure. Us fellows almost got into a fist fight, arguing over that." Bud snorted. "Whoever heard of a man being kidnapped by a monster?"

"I did," Grammy answered. "I attended a lecture given by a newspaper man who had talked to the

25

man who had been kidnapped. I also bought a book about it, probably the one Dick read. It's in the camper. You can read it tonight."

Bud shivered. "I'll have nightmares. Anyway, us fellows didn't fight because I said that by the time I returned home, I'd know whether Bigfoot was real or not. Do you think there's a real live monster up in the mountains where we're going?"

His grandmother chuckled. "I hope so."

"What'll we do if we see him?"

"Run like the dickens!" After a good laugh Grammy asked, "What do your parents think about the monster hunt?"

Bud wrinkled his nose. "Dad thinks it's a big joke. Mother thinks the hunt will be a beneficial learning experience." He gagged to show what he thought of beneficial learning experiences.

"Does your mother think such a monster might exist?"

His mother had explained the differences between man and ape, he said, but he'd forgotten most of what she said. "All I remember is, she told me not to be terribly disappointed if we didn't find a monster. She thinks probably it's a superbig bear. I had to promise not to fool around with any bears."

That was an excellent idea, Grammy mentioned. "Now, bring me up to date on everyone in the family."

Bud talked, and talked, and talked. Occasionally his grandmother chuckled, or said, "Well!" But never once did she interrupt, or correct his English.

He was still talking the next day when she turned off California State Highway 96 into a campground situated between the mouth of Bluff Creek and the Klamath River. After she switched off the motor, she suggested, "What say we open the camper windows so it will cool off inside, and then locate Mr. Ward?"

3
• • •

Carelessness Spells T-r-o-u-b-l-e

Mr. Ward was the biology teacher who had organized the monster hunt. Locating his campsite was easy since he had strung a lettered banner between two trees. It read WARD EXPEDITION. Bud was a little disappointed. He thought the banner should read MONSTER HUNT BEGINS HERE, like the clues his scoutmaster posted when the troop had a scavenger hunt. And, Bud noticed immediately, the people seated around a picnic table under the banner didn't look much like monster hunters. Four resembled middle-aged tourists. Three were young men with long hair and rings on their fingers. Another was a young woman with long hair and rings on her fingers. Then there was an ordinary looking fellow wearing faded blue jeans and a T-shirt and another dressed in an immaculate turtle-necked sweater and slacks.

Since Grammy had not met the leader, she announced, "I'm Matty Miller from San Diego. This is my grandson, Bud, from Boise, Idaho. Which of you is Mr. Ward?"

Brian Ward was the well-dressed young man. He welcomed them, and introduced Grammy and Bud to the others. Bud braced himself for the usual boring questions. However, no one asked how old he was, or what grade he was in school, or what he planned on being when he grew up.

"Are we the last ones to arrive?" Grammy inquired as she and Bud squeezed onto a bench. When they learned that two more parties were expected, Bud asked, "Are there going to be any kids my age?"

Mr. Ward informed Bud he was the only teenager. "But after we start searching for Bigfoot tomorrow, you won't be bored."

"I'm not bored," Bud protested. "I like camping in the mountains. I passed a course in wilderness survival given by the Boise Parks Department. It was so tough half the kids flunked."

Mr. Ward rubbed his hands. "Well! Aren't we fortunate to have an experienced mountain man in our group, folks! The rest of us are all city dudes, Bud. You'll tell us if we do something wrong, won't you?"

Bud's head swam. Having grownups look to him

for advice was like being beaned with a baseball. Actually, his secret worry was relieved. He feared Mr. Ward, being a biology teacher, would use lots of scientific words. He might even expect Bud to memorize the Latin names for pine trees, or chipmunks, or monsters. Suddenly an idea glowed in Bud's brain. If he knew the Latin word for monster, when he scribbled postcards to his pals at home, he could write, "Having a wonderful time hunting *Apeous horribileous*. Wish you were here. Your pal, Bud."

Even though the adults were chatting, Bud blurted out, "Mr. Ward! What's the scientific word for monster? *Apeous horribileous?*"

Mr. Ward silenced him with that special look teachers reserve for pupils who speak out of turn. The adults talked about where they were from, which mountain passes they had driven over to reach Bluff Creek, and how their pickup trucks, campers, vans, or motorcycles had performed on the winding steep roads. No one even mentioned the monster hunt. Finally Bud whispered loudly, "Hey, Gram, do I have to stick around here?"

Mr. Ward overheard the remark. "Why don't you go swimming?" He assured Bud's grandmother there was a safe place to swim in the Klamath River.

Grammy handed Bud the keys to the camper. Bud stood rooted to the ground, waiting to tune out the lecture that surely would follow: be careful; don't talk to strangers; don't lose the keys; don't stay in the water too long. Don't, don't, don't. Etc., etc., et cetera. At home his mother would have said all that, and more. But his grandmother had resumed talking with her new friends. He had nobody to tune out! By the time he reached the camper, selected the correct key on the ring and entered, he was chortling. Wow! What a vacation! No lectures, no nagging, no wisecracks from Larry or Pam. Wow, wow, wow!

With a whoop he emptied the contents of his duffel bag on the floor, donned swimming trunks and thongs, and bolted for the river. There he discovered that a sandbar mid-stream diverted the Klamath River's swift flow toward the far shore, while at the same time forming a natural pool along the near shore. Bud looked around eagerly for boys his age, but saw only one girl swimming in the deeper water. He dropped his towel and thongs, waded in and began to swim. But the water was so cold that he gasped for breath, dog-paddled a turn, and retreated to the pebbled beach. Already his teeth were rapping like drumsticks.

The girl swam toward him, submerged until her long black hair floated off her face, and stood up in waist-deep water. "Hi! Want to race to the end of the sandbar?"

Bud winced. He didn't even want to get wet again, let alone race a girl. But why let her think he couldn't swim? "Beat you!" he challenged. The girl waited until he splashed alongside her, and then sprinted. Bud flailed his arms and legs. By the time he reached the end of the pool, the girl was seated on the sandbar, wringing water out of her hair. Bud flopped down beside her, almost whinnying with relief as the sunbaked sand warmed his stomach and legs.

The girl repeated her greeting. "Hi! I'm Ella. Did you just come?"

"Y-y-yes," he answered through chattering teeth.

"Where from?"

"Boise, Idaho." Bud found it difficult to talk and control his shivering. Besides, he was embarrassed. Ella was a better swimmer than he was, and already deeply tanned. In comparison he felt he looked like a freshly plucked chicken.

"Day camp or overnight?"

"Huh?" It took a moment for Bud to understand that she was wondering if he had stopped for a swim on a drive through the canyon or would be camping overnight. "Overnight." Then he added importantly, "I'm with the Ward Expe . . . the Ward Scientific Expedition."

Ella made a face. "That bunch."

"What's the matter with 'that bunch'?" Bud demanded. "The expedition was organized to carry out a v-e-ry important scientific project."

Ella was not the least impressed. "Yeah, I know. We get scientific hunters through here all year. You're looking for that Bigfoot creature. So are a hundred other nuts."

Bud didn't know that. He had assumed the Ward Expedition was the only one. He'd even bragged to his pals that the leader had to obtain a license from the state, and negotiate a hunting treaty with the Indians, before the expedition was allowed to hunt Bigfoot. "Golly, I hope they don't capture him before we do."

This time Ella snorted. "Don't worry. They won't."

"How come you know so much?" Bud challenged.

Ella jackknifed to her feet. "I've got to go now. I work at the woodlot. Don't chop up any picnic tables if you need firewood. Come see me. I sell the stuff."

Bud detested vandalism and assured Ella he had never even carved his initials in a picnic table anywhere. The girl puzzled him. She had invited him to swim, but almost every other word from her was a put-down. "D'you live up here? I mean, all year round."

"All year round," she mimicked.

"I envy you, living right in the mountains. No wonder you're so brown already."

Ella's look was icier than the river. "I'm brown because I'm an Indian."

"Oh, par-don me! I thought you were a girl," Bud quipped, pleased at his snappy comeback. When Ella didn't laugh, he wondered if he had offended her. "Hey, look, I didn't mean—"

The girl cut him off. "I know. Some of your best friends are Indians."

Bud jerked to his feet and shoved out his chin. "Yeah! Some of my best friends *are* Indians. Where I live, half the kids in school are Indians or Chicanos or Blacks. It's no big deal!"

After an awkward silence, Ella slipped into the water like an otter, swam to the beach, and walked barefooted across the gravel into the trees.

Bud rapped his head with his knuckles, and talked to himself. Criminy, a fellow says something nice to a girl about her suntan, and what does he get? Nothing. Nought. Big fat zero. And now he had another freezing swim staring him in the face. After taking a deep breath, Bud plunged back into the river. On the beach he grabbed his towel and thongs and strode barefooted across the rocks. But after several painful steps he looked around to see if Ella was watching. Since she was not in sight, he slipped on the thongs. It wasn't his fault he had tender feet, he fumed to himself. His mother never let him go barefooted. She thought it was unsanitary.

From the path Bud noticed that Mr. Ward's campsite was deserted. Fearing the members had gone off to hunt without him, he hurried on. He was relieved to see his grandmother seated at the picnic table at their campsite. "I'm back," he announced. "Where is everybody?"

Grammy looked up from the book she was reading. "We recessed until after dinner. Did you have a nice swim?"

Bud nodded. "The water was freezing! I'm starved. Is lunch ready?"

It was not, his grandmother explained. She couldn't fix anything until he straightened the mess in the camper.

"Okay." Bud stepped the few paces from the table around to the rear of the camper. He stopped short. "Hey, Grammy, you left the camper door open. I almost bumped my nose ker-smash on it."

His grandmother replied calmly that she had not left the camper door open and the keys dangling in the lock. He had.

Bud made a great show of rapping his knuckles on his head. "Dumb me." He entered the camper, kicked off his thongs and tossed the towel on the table. As he reached for the clothing he had left in a heap, he gulped. His shirt was ripped to shreds!

There were large muddy pawprints on the floor, the table, and even the counter by the sink. Worst of all, the strap of his new tape recorder was badly chewed. Bud leaped to the ground, shouting, "Grammy, come look! A big dog got in the camper and tore everything to pieces!"

Grammy looked up from her book. "Yes, I know. Aren't you glad it was only a dog, and not a bear?"

"That's not funny! That dog chewed up my brand-new tape recorder!"

"I'm surprised you even have a tape recorder," she pointed out. "As a matter of fact, I'm surprised we still have a camper. Leaving the keys dangling in the door, and the door wide open was bound to cause trouble. Serious trouble. The camper could have been stolen."

For a moment Bud was panic-stricken. In the course he had taken on wilderness survival, he had learned that a careless, thoughtless person was not only a danger to himself, but to others. He knew it was sheer luck that a stranger hadn't spied the keys dangling in the open door, and either stolen articles or driven off the entire rig. And he was enormously relieved that a dog, and not a bear, had caused the mess. A bear could have totally wrecked the new camper. Still, he hated to admit he'd been a noodle-head. "I didn't know I was s'posed to lock the camper. I don't have to lock doors at home. You didn't tell me to lock the door and bring you the keys, the way Mom would."

Grammy sighed. "It never occurred to me that I'd have to think for you. So, march yourself into the camper, and clean up the mess."

Bud groaned. If there was one thing he hated more than anything, it was straightening up messes. But if he didn't do it, Grammy might be provoked enough to send him home! He hustled into the camper and looked for a place where he could shove everything out of sight. At home he could have kicked everything under the bed, or in the closet. But there wasn't a spare inch of storage space in the camper. It was really different, kind of like a . . . a . . . Last night, before he went to sleep, he had pretended it was a four-wheeled space vehicle carrying a brave two-man crew out to explore the world of a mysterious monster. He'd even imagined his name was Armstrong Moonwalker Miller. And Grammy's name was Aldrina. Of course, everyone aboard the real spaceship was a heads-up, work-together team player. No one aboard *Eagle* left the door open, or keys dangling. So, if he wanted his grandmother to think he was a Number One Somebody instead of the Number Five Nobody in the Miller family, he'd better shape up.

"Get going, Miller," he ordered himself sternly. Straightening the camper wasn't difficult. Next,

Bud decided to surprise Grammy by fixing lunch. Then he had a stupendous idea. To get out of saying "I'm sorry," he'd make a sandwich with a *message*. Chortling, Bud opened the refrigerator and brought out cold meat, pickles, a hard-boiled egg, tomato, lettuce, cheese, onion, and mustard. Soon the man-sized sandwiches were assembled on plates and glasses of milk poured. Next Bud printed the words I'M SORRY on a paper napkin and laid it atop his grandmother's sandwich. Then he called, "Lunch is ready. Come 'n' get it!"

The moment Grammy stepped inside, she enthused, "My, you really did clean up the mess. And you fixed lunch." When she read Bud's message, tears came to her eyes. She hugged Bud, and put the napkin in a drawer. "That goes in my Memory Scrapbook. Only very special treasures are saved for that."

"Aw, it's not that great," Bud replied as a hard knot of worry dissolved in his stomach. "The sandwich is more special."

"Then let's eat," Grammy suggested as she slid onto her seat beside the table. After peeking at the filling, she chuckled, "Now I won't have to clean out the refrigerator."

After a few bites Bud found the courage to say, "I sure acted like a noodlehead. I know better."

Grammy patted his hand. "Well, I guess everyone is entitled to one goof."

4
• • •

A Monster Hunter Needs
Plenty of Snuff

After he finished lunch Bud asked, "Are we going to do anything special this afternoon? Did any more people arrive?"

None had, Grammy informed him. Mr. Ward gave those present a list of supplies each should have on hand before going up the Bluff Creek road the next day—items such as food, propane gas, gasoline, flashlight batteries, and so on. These were available at a store farther down the highway. "I'm going to take a nap. If you're not sleepy, why don't you start reading that book on monsters I bought?"

Bud grimaced. "I don't have to read about Bigfoot to know what we're looking for."

"Maybe so. But have you forgotten how Grampy always studied a mining area before his company sent him out to judge whether millions should be invested in developing the mineral resources? Even though he was an expert in his field, Grampy always made the effort to learn more. Well, I'm no expert on monsters, so I decided I'd better do some studying. That's why I bought the book."

Reading a book wasn't his idea of hunting for a hairy man-ape, Bud declared. Couldn't his grandmother just tell him what was in the book? Would he have to read it? He wasn't too hot on science. Science was his weakest subject, he confessed, after grammar and spelling.

Grammy understood. However, one chapter was so exciting that she knew Bud would be disappointed if he didn't read it. "It's about a man named Albert Ostman, a prospector in British Columbia. He claimed he was kidnapped by a Sasquatch." Then she added that up in British Columbia and the state of Washington, people called monsters Sasquatch instead of Bigfoot.

Bud gasped. "That kidnapping really happened? My pal Dick said he read about it in a library book. I thought he was kidding. Sure, I'll read that."

As soon as Grammy lay down, Bud opened the book. While skimming through the pages in search of Albert Ostman's name, he read that the word

"Sasquatch" was the English version of *Sasq'atl* or *Soss q'atl*, a term used by Indians to describe hairy two-legged wild creatures long encountered in the wilds of British Columbia and Vancouver Island, in westernmost Canada. The word meant "wild man of the woods." The first white man to record seeing the creature was Alexander Caulfield Anderson, a fur trader for the Hudson's Bay Company. While pioneering a trade route through the Rocky Mountains and along the Fraser River in present-day British Columbia in 1864, Anderson reported in his journal that "hairy humanoids" hurled rocks down on his party.

Bud guessed "humanoids" meant that the creatures had some human characteristics. Since there were no scary details of an actual man-and-beast struggle, he read on. The next incident described happened in July, 1884. According to a news item in *The Daily British Colonist* published then at Victoria, on Vancouver Island, a creature described as a "gorilla" had been captured near Lytton, British Columbia. The half-man, half-beast was about four feet, seven inches tall, weighed 127 pounds, and resembled a human being. However, his body, excluding his hands and feet, was covered with dark hair. The newspaper report mentioned that the captors nicknamed the extraordinary creature "Jacko," and planned to exhibit him in London,

England. But, the author stated, nothing more was ever heard of Jacko or his captors. To this day, no one knew if the reported capture was a hoax, or whether Jacko was a gorilla, a chimpanzee, or a wild man.

Bud leaned back and closed his eyes. He imagined he was the one who single-handedly captured the Jacko creature. Gosh-all-gollee, maybe he could do the same right here in northern California! Why not? If he had a long rope, and some kind of bait— candy, or raw carrots, or hamburger. Sure, hamburger! Raw meat! The very thing. He opened his eyes, and told himself to ask Grammy to buy lots of hamburger. Then he leafed through more pages until he came to the story of Albert Ostman.

As a young man Albert Ostman had worked as a logger and carpenter in the fall, winter, and spring. Every summer he prospected for gold in the heavily timbered, rugged mountains of British Columbia. Thus it was not unusual for him to decide, in 1924, to venture alone into the wilds surrounding Toba Inlet, on the coast. Accordingly, he traveled by steamer to Lund, a small port. There he hired an Indian to transport him and his gear by boat to the head of the inlet. During the trip the guide assured him that gold had been discovered in the area. He knew of one prospector who appeared at Lund with a rawhide poke heavy with nuggets. After squandering his new riches in gambling and drinking, he disappeared into the mountains, only to reappear weeks later with more gold. This happened repeatedly. Never once did the miner reveal the location of his rich strike, nor was anyone able to trail him there. When he failed to return one season, groups organized to search for him and his gold mine. Neither was ever found. The Indian guide concluded his tale by saying that his people felt that *Soss q'atl* had killed the prospector.

Ostman was familiar with tales about *Soss q'atl,* the "wild man of the woods," but he didn't believe the creature really existed. Even though the guide insisted *Soss q'atl* was real, Ostman felt no qualms about prospecting alone. His marksmanship with a rifle had saved him more than once in a harrowing encounter with a bear or enraged moose.

The guide left Ostman at the mouth of a creek, promising to return in three weeks. Ostman set up camp, killed a deer for meat, and prospected the lower reaches of the stream. Finding no gold, he shouldered an eighty-pound pack and followed the creek far up into the mountains. Days passed as he prospected one creek drainage after another. One evening he made camp near a spring. As a usual precautionary measure against bears and porcupines, he hung his knapsack from a tree limb, and slept with his boots inside his sleeping bag. The next morning he found the contents of the knapsack spilled on the ground, and a package of dried fruit missing. Since the other contents were not damaged, Ostman figured that a porcupine, not a bear, had prowled the camp. That night he slept with his rifle and hunting knife inside the sleeping bag.

The next thing he knew, Ostman later reported, "I was wakened by something picking me up." Whoever it was, was walking! Painfully cramped in the sleeping bag, Ostman could not get at his knife or rifle. He knew that no ordinary man, even a tough strong logger, could carry another adult male with such ease while obviously climbing a steep mountain slope. So, either he had been grabbed by a man of extraordinary strength and size, or by a *Soss q'atl*.

Ostman was not in doubt for long. The creature finally dropped him on the ground. Ostman struggled out of his bag. When his eyes adjusted to the star-bright night, he found himself facing not one, but four huge hairy manlike beasts: an adult male about eight feet tall with broad shoulders, an adult female, and a younger male and female. A *Soss q'atl* family! The creatures jabbered among themselves, and suddenly withdrew.

Ostman speedily donned his boots, and sat, with rifle ready, until the early morning light dispelled the darkness. He was in a small clearing surrounded by mountains. The only way in and out was through a narrow opening in the rocks. Unfortunately for him, the creatures settled themselves between Ostman and his gateway to freedom.

Ostman's intense curiosity overrode his first alarm. He figured that to escape alive, he must remain calm, and if possible, make friends with his hairy hosts. So, with astonishing control, he set up camp. Fortunately his captor had brought along Ostman's knapsack. Ostman took inventory, and was relieved to find he had enough tinned meat, crackers, and coffee to last about a week. Even better, he had six rifle shells, matches, and several small containers of snuff. Moving slowly, Ostman gathered wood, started a fire, and ate sparingly. Then he treated himself to a pinch of finely powdered snuff, and settled back to watch the family gather grass, leaves, and grubs for its meal.

Whenever Ostman walked about, always with rifle in hand, some member of the family followed at a distance. But either the adult male or female guarded the V-shaped opening in the mountainside. At dark the family withdrew to the shelter of overhanging rocks beside the opening. Ostman spent the night keeping his fire going, and dozing.

By this time he felt he had only two choices: one, kill at least the adult creatures, which he was reluctant to do because they fascinated him; two, trick them somehow so that he could escape unharmed. But how to trick the *Soss q'atl?* After much thought he remembered hearing about a man who escaped a maddened bull by blinding it with snuff. Maybe he could do that, too! At least it was worth a try.

For the next few days Ostman quietly coaxed the young male to approach close enough so he could toss him a bit of meat or cracker, and always a half-emptied tin of snuff. The young one licked the tobacco dust instead of putting a small pinch up his nostrils, and carried the container to his father, who also relished the taste. After several such offerings Ostman wakened one morning to find the adult and young males sitting a mere ten feet away. Again, slowly and with great calm, he started his small cook-fire, filled the coffee tin with water from the spring, and set the can to boiling. He ate meat and crackers, smacking his lips often. As he opened a fresh container of snuff, the adult male snatched it away and tongued its entire contents into his mouth. When the strong tobacco burned his tongue, he grabbed the coffee can, which Ostman had set aside to cool, and drained its contents. For a moment the creature seemed gratified. But suddenly his eyes watered. He gasped, squealed, and loped toward the spring, with the younger one at his heels. When the female also raced for the spring to help her mate, Ostman dashed for the opening. He escaped, sped down-mountain, and two days later limped into a logging camp. From there he made his way to his home in Vancouver. Fearful of the ridicule that would be heaped on him if he publicized his encounter with the *Soss q'atl,* Ostman remained silent for over twenty-five years. At long last he wrote an account which brought him small fame as the only white man known to have survived being kidnapped by the creatures now called Sasquatch.

Bud put down the book slowly. He had held his breath while reading the final page, and was panting.

Grammy had wakened, and asked, "What's the matter?"

Bud pleaded, "Grammy, can we go to the store right now and buy some cans of snuff?"

5

• • •

Double-talk About *Omah*

The next morning Bud was wakened before daylight by the sound of a truck leaving the campground. "Grammy, we better get up! They're leaving without us!"

Grammy parted the curtains and looked out. Her bed was at the front of the camper, on a raised platform supported by the roof of the truck cab. "That's probably a fisherman. Remember, Mr. Ward said we'd all leave together between nine and ten."

"Oh, yeah. I forgot." Bud snuggled back into his sleeping bag. It was laid out on the cushions used in the daytime as seats on each side of the table. Although he tried to go back to sleep, his stomach gurgled repeatedly. "Can I get something to eat?"

Grammy approved. "Good idea. How about fixing a bowl of cereal for me, too?"

Bud wriggled out and switched on the light over the sink. "Want me to heat water for instant cocoa?"

Grammy sighed blissfully. "Wonderful! It's just like old times with Grampy. He always served me breakfast in bed. Of course, breakfast might be at 3:00 A.M., and the camper cold as ice, but he always treated me like a queen."

"Cereal and cocoa coming up, Your Majesty," Bud announced. He handed Grammy her bowl and perched on the edge of his bed to eat. "This is all right for a starter, but can I make pancakes later on?" He had made certain his grandmother stocked a plentiful supply of pancake mix.

She nodded, and then asked how sleepy he was.

Bud yawned noisily. "I dunno. Why?"

"Before sunup is the best time to see wildlife. What about leaving now, instead of later?"

The previous evening Mr. Ward announced he would lead the expedition caravan up the Bluff Creek road. There would be frequent stops at places where Bigfoot had been sighted, or his giant-sized footprints found.

Grammy continued, "If we drive very slowly, we're certain to see some deer and elk."

Bud grinned. "And maybe Bigfoot!"

49

Grammy chortled. "Keep your fingers crossed—and your camera ready."

As soon as the water boiled, Bud spooned cocoa mix into their mugs. But at that moment someone knocked on the camper door. Bud looked questioningly at his grandmother.

"Who's there?" Grammy called out.

A voice answered softly, "It's me. Ella."

"Ella?" Grammy whispered to Bud.

"The girl I met swimming." He had told Grammy about her.

"Invite her to come in."

Bud grimaced. "I'm in my pajamas!" He scrambled into his sleeping bag and pulled it up to his chin.

"Com-ing," Grammy called out. She lowered herself to the floor and padded barefooted to the door. The moment she saw the thin long-haired girl, she smiled. "Good morning, Ella. I'm Bud's grandmother, Mrs. Miller. Come in."

Ella shook her head. "I guessed you were awake because a light was on. I . . . I came over to apologize because my Dad's truck woke you up so early."

"Oh, don't apologize. We planned to get up early," Grammy assured her. "Come in! Bud was . . . I was just fixing some hot cocoa. Won't you join us?"

Ella hesitated. "You've probably got lots to do."

50

"We're never too busy for company. Come in!"

Ella climbed the steps. "Hi," she mumbled at Bud, curled up in the farthest corner of the bed cushions.

"Hi," he mumbled back.

Grammy gently pressed Ella to sit on the edge of a cushion. While fixing a third mug of cocoa, she asked, "Do you get up this early every morning?"

Ella said it was her job to fix her father's breakfast and pack his lunch bucket. "He hauls logs out of Bluff Creek."

"That's where we're going today," Bud informed her.

Grammy handed Bud and Ella their cocoa, and then seated herself cross-legged on a cushion. "We're leaving ahead of the others, so we can see some deer or elk along the road."

"Or Bigfoot," Bud replied a little testily.

Ella ignored Bud. She blew on the cocoa and sipped carefully. "Thanks, Mrs. Miller. This tastes good." As she drank, she looked about the camper. Then suddenly she pulled a crumpled five-dollar bill from her jacket pocket and laid it on the cushion at Grammy's feet. "I'm sorry my dog made such a mess. That's to pay for the shirt he ripped up."

Bud's mouth gaped. *"Your* dog?"

Ella kept her chin up. "When I came back from swimming, I whistled, and he came out of here. I looked in, but I didn't touch a thing. I sat on the steps until I saw you coming. Then I left."

Grammy picked up the money and put it in her pajama pocket. But she withdrew it immediately and placed the bill on Ella's knee. "Your dog was not at fault. The door was open. There was no one here to tell him to go away. Thank you for guarding our camper."

Ella's dark eyes shone as she pocketed the money. "Now it's all right?"

Grammy nodded. "Now we are friends. You are our guest."

Bud had watched the two closely. There was something he didn't understand, but he wasn't going to let on. "I'm glad you came," he said so sincerely that Ella looked straight at him for the first time, and smiled.

Grammy continued the conversation. "Bud told me you live here all year round."

Ella pointed with her thumb. "In that trailer parked by the woodlot. My Dad cuts the wood. I sell it."

"Where's your mother?" Bud inquired.

The girl ignored his question. "I've got an older brother. He's up on the mountain looking after the Old One."

"Your grandfather?" Grammy guessed.

"Great-grandfather. Every summer we have to

take him up there so he can live the old way." She chewed her lip, and then jerked her thumb at Bud. "He says you're hunting Bigfoot, but I don't see any gun rack in here. Where're your guns?"

Grammy explained that she and Bud hunted only with binoculars and cameras.

"You don't want to kill that Bigfoot?"

Kill Bigfoot! Bud and Grammy said they never thought of such a thing. No one in their expedition meant to kill Bigfoot. The most anyone hoped for was to take photographs of the creature.

"Then why so many guns and rope?" Ella demanded. "That leader fellow and his helpers! They've got guns and rope." Then she shrugged. "They won't find nothin'."

"Ella thinks Bigfoot is a big joke," Bud informed Grammy.

Grammy's eyes twinkled as she asked Ella solemnly, "You have never seen the creature called Bigfoot?"

"No, ma'am," Ella answered politely. But her lips trembled as if she was trying not to laugh. "Hoopa Indians never see the creature Bigfoot."

Grammy leaned forward. "What does the Old One see?"

Ella's cheeks flushed. Suddenly she drained her mug, placed it on the counter, and stepped to the door. "If you want to find out about *Omah,* maybe

53

the Old One will tell you." She left so quickly neither Bud nor his grandmother could say good-bye.

Bud exhaled noisily and slumped against the wall. "Well, how do you like that?"

Grammy chuckled. "I like that very much. Ella is a fine girl."

Bud wrinkled his nose. Ella had a chip on her shoulder. "What was that rigamarole over the five-dollar bill? Criminy, the way we were sitting around cross-legged in a circle, you'd think we were having a powwow in a wigwam!"

"That's exactly what we were doing!" Grammy explained that Ella was deeply embarrassed because her dog had entered the camper uninvited and damaged their belongings. Apparently she had learned from her parents that people do not go uninvited into a friend's or a stranger's house, nor destroy other people's things. To her way of thinking, she had lost face and must make amends.

"But you gave the money back," Bud protested.

Grammy said she had to accept the money. "I pocketed it to show Ella I was satisfied, and bore her no ill will. That way she regained face. Then, by assuring her that she did us a favor by guarding the camper against further intruders, I let her know we were in her debt. When I placed the money on her person, she accepted it as a gift."

"A gift?" Bud exploded. "She just took back her own money!"

Bud was confused because he didn't understand Indians, Grammy explained further. The moment Ella laid the money at Grammy's feet it was no longer Ella's. It belonged to the injured party, the one whose property was damaged. But when Grammy, the property owner, offered Ella that money in return for Ella's protecting the camper, it was proper for Ella to accept it as payment for a service rendered. "The score was even. We could be friends with neither one obligated to the other."

Bud rolled his eyes. "Yeah, but I'm still out a brand-new shirt. Do we give up looking for Bigfoot just because Ella thinks Bigfoot is a big joke?"

Grammy shook her head. "Ella didn't say that. You did."

"She told you she had never seen Bigfoot. She said Hoopa Indians never saw Bigfoot either."

Grammy smiled as she pointed out, "No, Ella didn't say that. Think, now. I asked if she had ever seen the creature *called* Bigfoot. Right?"

"And she said no," Bud interrupted. "And then she mumbled something about *Omah* and to ask her great-grandfather. Yech! We're supposed to spend all summer looking for an old Indian instead of a real live monster!"

"Now, simmer down," Grammy cautioned. She

leaned back and folded her hands around her empty mug. "I don't blame you for being confused. The same thing happened to Grampy and me when we stayed with Indians for the first time. We listened to them with our white men's ears. It took us a long, long time to listen with our minds . . . to search out what they were really saying. For instance, what Ella really said was that Hoopa Indians never see the creature *white men call* Bigfoot. That's the truth, to their way of thinking. The answer hinges on the word, Bigfoot. Of course, Hoopas don't see a creature called Bigfoot. They see one with an Indian name, *Omah!* And, as I figure it, by telling us to ask the Old One about *Omah,* Ella was admitting her people do know about a creature named *Omah.*"

Bud jiggled excitedly. "Then there *is* a monster!"

Grammy warned he was jumping to conclusions. *Omah* could be a real live wild creature. But more likely, *Omah* was a spirit creature about whom the tribe wove fanciful legends. "If we want to learn the true meaning of the word, we have to first find her great-grandfather. But remember, she didn't promise he would tell us anything. She was challenging us."

Bud eyed his grandmother warily. "Challenging us?"

"To listen to what Indians say. White men don't have all the answers. They don't know all there is

56

to know about the creature. And another thing, if Ella didn't believe we had no intention of harming *Omah,* I doubt she ever would have revealed the name. Not only did she confide this special bit of knowledge, she trusted us not to tell Mr. Ward and the others. You see, Indians don't kill wild things for sport, the way white hunters do. At least, they didn't used to kill for sport, though nowadays it's hard to tell some Indians from white men. But do you understand now why you have to take time to think about what an Indian says?"

Bud guessed so. However, no matter whether the monster was called Bigfoot or *Omah* or Siss-boom-bah, Bud believed the monster was real. Look what happened to Albert Ostman! And what about that photograph in the book, snapped somewhere near the headwaters of Bluff Creek? That showed a real live monster.

Photographs can be faked, Grammy pointed out. However, from all she had read, the one filmed on Bluff Creek was not a fake. Many people believed it was the best piece of evidence ever gathered proving that Bigfoot, or that kind of monster, really existed. Still other people, including scientists, refused to believe what they saw in the photograph.

"Then who do we believe?" Bud cried out, obviously upset.

Grammy patted his arm. "Young man, what's the

matter with your curiosity bump? Give it a hard rub. Make it itch! Like Grampy used to do when he was faced with a tough question. Are you going to be satisfied with what people tell you, or what you read in a book or see on television? Don't you want to find out all you can about this big mystery, and then make up your own mind what you think is the correct answer?"

"What if I guess wrong?" Bud worried aloud. Larry and Pam and Doug and everybody would laugh him off the planet.

"What if you guess right?"

Without realizing it, Bud had started rapping his head with his knuckles. Golly-gee-gosh, what if he did guess right? What if he found out something on his very own . . . like, maybe finding Bigfoot himself!

Grammy interrupted his thoughts by asking if his curiosity bump had started to itch yet.

Bud giggled. "It's itching like the dickens!" He wriggled out of his sleeping bag. "Come on! Let's get going up the mountain!"

6

• • •

Bigfoot Country

Bud grabbed his clothes and dressed quickly in the small bathroom at the rear of the camper. When he emerged in sixty seconds, his grandmother looked disgusted. Bud gulped, and popped back inside before his grandmother reminded him that he had a short memory. Very short. Yesterday, on the drive to the store for snuff, pancake mix, and other necessities, Grammy had talked about sharing the work and fun of a monster hunt. There were daily chores to be done, inside and outside the camper, in camp and on the hunt. "Right?"

"Right!" Bud agreed heartily.

On the drive back to the campground Grammy had outlined clearly what she expected Bud to do every day, without having to be nagged. This included making his bed, picking up his clothes, brushing his teeth, and combing his hair. She expected him to look like a grandson, not an uncombed, unwashed junior wild man. Bud raised his right hand and took a Boy Scout oath not to forget.

Now, behind the bathroom door he looked himself squarely in the eye in the mirror. "You got a memory like a sieve, Miller. Get smart." He undressed, washed, brushed his teeth, dressed, combed his hair, and even put the cap back on the tube of toothpaste.

When he reappeared, Grammy smiled. "That's more like it." She handed him the key ring. "It's lighter outside. I don't think you'll need the flashlight."

Bud's next chore was already his favorite. Grammy had taught him how to start the truck properly, and adjust the choke so the motor would idle smoothly. Unfortunately this did not include racing the motor, nor making the exhaust backfire. Still, Grammy assured him that learning to handle the switches, gears, and hand-choke on a well-aged, four-wheel-drive pickup was practically a lost art. If he proved he could be trusted, she would teach him how to drive the rig. For Bud, this was almost as exciting as hunting a monster. At least he would have something to brag about if he returned home empty-handed, without a hank of monster hair or a plaster cast of a giant-sized footprint.

After unlocking the cab door and settling himself in the driver's seat, Bud rehearsed each step in his mind. Then, twiddling his fingers like a man robbing a safe on television, he unlocked the ignition, stepped on the starter, and fingered the choke button cautiously. When the motor started on the first try, he congratulated himself. While the motor idled, he cleaned the windshield, mirrors, and exterior lights, checked the fuel and water lines for leaks, and retracted the hydraulic stabilizer jacks.

Grammy leaned out the rear door and called, "Are we ready to roll?"

Bud offered a snappy salute. "Everything checked, Captain. Ready to roll."

"Binoculars in the cab? Camera?"

Bud nodded. "Where's the map?"

"Oops, the Captain almost forgot." Grammy retrieved the map and her pocketbook, and locked the door behind her.

While there was enough early light to see the trees and shrubs close by, Grammy had to switch the headlights on dim in order to drive. She and Bud rolled down the windows and watched in the rearview mirrors as she backed out of the campsite. Then she shifted gears and eased out of the campground onto the highway.

"We forgot something," Bud remembered. "We didn't leave a note for Mr. Ward."

"It's all right. I told him last night we might ?ave early. He marked the map so I know where ur headquarters will be up on the mountain."

Three hundred yards to the south she cornered off :he State Highway onto the Bluff Creek road. It was paved and wide enough to accommodate two-way logging truck traffic. In the first few miles they passed several turnouts occupied by vans and campers.

"Are all those people hunting Bigfoot, too?"

Grammy thought more likely they were fishermen.

"Ella told me lots of people were hunting Bigfoot. Did you know that? Were you surprised when she said Mr. Ward and his friends brought guns? Couldn't they get us into trouble?" Bud worried aloud.

Any person caught shooting wildlife out of season would be breaking the law. However, there was no law forbidding people from carrying guns for their personal protection while camping or hiking in the forest. That included while searching for monsters. Deer and elk were no threat, but bears were always dangerous. Bud knew his grandfather's guns were hidden in a locked compartment in the camper. Grammy would carry one whenever she thought it necessary, so he wasn't worried about bears attacking them, or mountain lions dropping down onto them. Having a grandmother who was a crack shot was very reassuring. "I've been wondering. Are we all going to hunt Bigfoot together? I mean, do we have to stick with a crowd? I was hoping you and I could stalk him on our own."

Grammy grinned. "We'll see how things work out."

Her answer didn't quite satisfy Bud. "Can I say something? I know kids aren't supposed to criticize grownups, but I don't like Mr. Ward. Even before Ella blabbed about the guns and rope, he turned me off. Do you like him?"

Grammy remarked that kids definitely should not criticize grownups, or anyone, until they had good reason. While she felt Mr. Ward might be more at home in a classroom than the forest, she was prepared to like him for the time being. "Now, let's stop talking and watch for animals."

The road followed the meanderings of the creek. However, since the right-of-way had been bulldozed through virgin growth, it resembled a tunnel walled with towering pine, cedar, and madrona trees, and dense undergrowth. Bud leaned out the window to inhale the rich strong aroma of centuries-old timber and ground litter of dead leaves, needles, cones, and broken branches. Occasionally he glimpsed reflections of small creatures' eyes in the dim headlights.

The steady low hum of the engine and the low-beam lights caused no alarm among the deer grazing along the roadway. Some remained poised until the camper was very close, and then with fluid grace bounded out of sight.

Within a half hour visibility improved, so Grammy turned off the lights. When the paved segment of the road ended, they continued on a graveled surface. Bud pointed at the rearview mirror on his side. "Look at the dust we're kicking up, and we're not driving fast. I'm glad we're not driving in that caravan." The shrubbery alongside the road was so coated with dust that Bud was positive Bigfoot wouldn't be lurking there. Although the road and forest remained in deep shadow, the sky was turning pink. Bud continued to hang over the door, straining for a glimpse of a big dark furry object. Finally he tired and leaned back on his seat. "No sign of Bigfoot yet."

Grammy chuckled. "You can't expect action this soon. It's not like watching television."

"I know . . . but wouldn't it be great if we spotted a huge dark thing up ahead, and it really was Bigfoot? Wow, wow, wow!" Bud closed his eyes and imagined the scene. Suddenly he squawked, "Criminy, the binoculars are still in the case, and I haven't set my camera!" He busied himself readying both for action. "Honest, now, Grammy . . . what will you do if Bigfoot appears?"

Grammy guessed she would do the same as the people she read about in the book. All reacted similarly whenever a huge hairy creature unexpectedly appeared beside the road. They pressed hard on the horn to scare the beast, and stomped the accelerator pedal to the floor. She scratched her chin. "On second thought, I'd roll up the window before I honked the horn."

Bud studied the door handle on his side. He rolled the window up and down as quickly as he could. "Yeah, rolling up the window first would be smart. Then, even if Bigfoot ran alongside the camper, he couldn't reach in and grab you or me with his claws."

Hands, not claws, Grammy corrected him. Bigfoot was said to have hands and feet similar to humans.

Bud spread wide the fingers of his right hand. "How much bigger?"

"Two, maybe three, times bigger, if we encountered a fully grown adult."

Bud giggled nervously. He rolled the window up and down again. "Not fast enough. You know what we should have? A squirt gun filled with soapsuds or ammonia water. We should have bought one at the store. I could keep it right here on my lap, and squirt Bigfoot in the face before he got his hand on the door."

Making a squirt gun was no problem. Grammy promised to find something to serve the purpose. Up in the mountains and far from a store, you made do with what you had.

The road curved more and more now, skirting timbered gulches threaded with the run-off from spring-fed creeks emerging high on the mountains closing in on both sides. Soon the road began to climb in a series of switchbacks gouged through timber or blasted from the steepening slopes. Bluff Creek was now several hundred feet below the road, and hidden by trees. A cat's cradle of dirt roads cleared for transporting logs scarred the slopes. But since each exit was marked by a sign bearing a number, and these numbers were noted on the map furnished by Mr. Ward, Grammy had no concern about getting lost. At length they came into an area where the lemon-yellow rays of early sunlight flooded a small meadow and creek. Grammy stopped on the log bridge spanning the water. "We shouldn't hurry past such a beautiful scene."

Bud leaned over the steering wheel to view the downward course of the creek. "Let's hike down there. Maybe we'll find some monster footprints!"

Grammy checked the map. "We're still about ten miles from where Bigfoot has actually been sighted. But let's give it a go anyway." She moved the camper onto a turnout, and then snorted disgustedly. "Fishermen!" she observed, pointing to the litter of beer cans, trash, and cigarette butts. From the shelf behind her she unfolded a sturdy plastic bag. "Let's clean up the worst of the mess." She rolled up her window, and advised Bud to do the same.

"What for? Nobody's around."

If Bigfoot should lunge out of the forest, and they had to run for their lives, they'd be better off if the windows were raised. "Unless you plan on standing stock-still until he comes up to you, and shakes hands."

Bud eyed the door and window handles. "Remind me to oil them tonight."

The two stepped down onto the road, stretched, and filled their lungs with the clean cedar-spiced air. Then both darted about, picking up trash. Within five minutes the parking area looked cleaner, and the bag was half-full. Grammy tossed it in the cab, and led the way to the creek. Since it was narrow, shallow, and emerald clear, she and Bud checked the near and far banks for tracks. They found many made by deer, porcupine, mice, and fishermen.

"Aw, shucks." Bud voiced his disappointment as they strolled back across the flower-studded meadow. "We're so far up in the mountains, I was sure we'd spot something."

Once more Grammy reminded him that no one knew for certain whether a creature like Bigfoot really existed.

67

Bud studied the forest surrounding them, shielding his eyes from the sunlight. "I know, but I don't care. I believe in Bigfoot. But why does he always run away? What is it about people that frightens him? He's bigger than we are, and can run faster."

Of course, Bud knew the answer. Bigfoot was a wild creature. Instinctively he was wary of other creatures in his domain, until he learned they posed no threat to his well-being. Still Bud murmured wistfully, "Bigfoot could have tramped across this meadow, couldn't he? He could have drunk from that creek, couldn't he?"

Grammy's eyes twinkled. "He could be watching us from behind a tree right this very minute!"

Bud snapped his fingers. "We better run!"

The two raced to the truck, vaulted inside the cab, and slammed their doors. "I beat!" Bud shouted, laughing. "That was fun. And you know what? We should practice doing this, a lot. We have to be prepared for . . ." he rolled his eyes, ". . . you-know-what!"

Grammy was too winded to talk. She rolled down her window, pressed the starter, and continued on up the road.

Another half hour's drive brought them alongside an ugly logged-off clearing on the right, or upmountain, side of the road. Delapidated shacks, tents, and a half dozen trailers and campers were scattered amidst sawed-off tree trunks, weeds, and unsightly trash. No one was stirring about, nor any cookfires blazing, yet the camp was obviously inhabited. "Loggers' camp, probably," she guessed. "Three or four more miles, and we should be right about where all the Bigfoot excitement began."

Shortly after she pulled off the road onto a turnout, and parked the rig. "Here we are, Bud, right smack dab in real Bigfoot country. What say we snoop around?"

"Okay!" Bud whooped. "Bigfoot, here we come!"

7

• • •

The Hunt Begins

Bud scurried like a squirrel along the edges of the road. He darted right and left, off the shoulder, across the road and back, searching for monster prints in the soft dirt. Again he was disappointed.

Grammy patted his shoulder. "Remember, from the time we left Portland, I cautioned you that the Bigfoot story could be a hoax. But are you going to give up this soon?"

"There isn't a smidgeon of a print anywhere," he argued stubbornly. "If this is such an important place, why isn't there a marker reading BIGFOOT WAS HERE?"

The evening before Bud had read about the first of many Bigfoot sightings along Bluff Creek. Back in August, 1958, a bulldozer operator was clearing brush at this point on a road construction project. He discovered sixteen-inch-long footprints resembling those of a barefooted, five-toed human. The man's fellow workers believed the tracks were made by a "wild man" they'd heard about for years. A news story about the mysterious tracks appeared in *The Humboldt Times,* published over the mountain at Eureka, California. The headline read HUGE FOOTPRINTS HOLD MYSTERY OF FRIENDLY BLUFF CREEK GIANT. Within a week the story was reprinted in newspapers across the country. Readers were delighted with it. Hundreds even rushed to Bluff Creek, eager to capture what they felt must be America's *yeti,* or Abominable Snowman. However, since the northern California mountains are free of snow ten months of the year, the term "snowman" was not appropriate. One reporter coined a catchier phrase, *Big Foot,* soon shortened to *Bigfoot.*

The local excitement skyrocketed when two other construction workers actually sighted a wild hairy apelike monster at least seven feet tall. Although they shot at it, and set their hunting dogs to run it down, the creature vanished in the forest. Until snowfall, monster hunters thronged the surrounding region, but none glimpsed Bigfoot. The following spring Bigfoot obligingly ranged the upper Bluff Creek drainage, leaving enough tracks to drive hunters into a tizzy. That August a well-known naturalist arrived to conduct a serious study of the Bigfoot evidence. This expert, Ivan T. Sanderson, had devoted years to gathering material on monsters reportedly seen in northern India, Russia, and the Himalaya Mountains. Since Bigfoot prowled upper Bluff Creek still another time, Mr. Sanderson made plaster casts of the fresh footprints. He considered these the most important monster evidence ever found, much more so than the snowy prints photographed in the Himalayas.

However, the biggest excitement about Bigfoot had occurred in October, 1967, when a rancher named Roger Patterson not only encountered Bigfoot, but obtained a color-film sequence of this fearsome-looking, apelike creature as it loped across a sunlit clearing near Bluff Creek. Experts strove to prove the photograph was faked. They claimed the creature was only a tall man costumed in a monkey suit. Most viewers disagreed. No doubt about it, they declared stoutly, this proved Bigfoot was real! Actually some scientists felt the photograph superceded the footprints as the best evidence ever obtained of the mysterious monster's actual existence.

Even though Bud knew all this had happened close to where he was standing, he still looked glum. To cheer him, Grammy reminded him that animal tracks got washed out during a rainfall or, in hot dry weather, crumbled into dust. "You mustn't feel badly just because you can't find any tracks here." After all, large wild creatures ranged over a wide territory in search of food. If they could find none in one area, they sought another. Also, if they encountered too many threats to their lives and privacy in one place, they withdrew to a safer one.

"I know all that," Bud interrupted impatiently. "I've read about bears and apes and other animals which migrate hundreds of miles every year searching for food."

Grammy dug her fists into her ribs. "Hmmph! Roger Patterson searched eight years—*eight years!*—before he snapped that photograph of Bigfoot. Here you are, pouting like a two-year-old because you haven't got the critter pinned to the ground in ten minutes!"

The notion of wrestling Bigfoot to the ground was so ridiculous that Bud burst out laughing. "Okay, okay."

The two drove higher into the mountains. At long last they reached another logged-off clearing. Grammy checked the map to make certain this was where the expedition would establish its headquarters.

Bud's lips curled. "Some dump!"

A camper and a tent already occupied ground by a creek. It cascaded down the mountainside, disappeared into a culvert under the road, and gushed forth on the lower side. The camper and tent appeared to be deserted. While Grammy looked for a place to park her rig, a logging truck swung into sight around a curve farther up the road. The driver shattered the stillness by honking the horn. Grammy quickly eased the camper along the rutted wheel tracks leading into the campground. Seconds later the heavy ten-wheeled truck transporting a pyramid of logs thundered past, spewing dust in every direction.

"I wonder if that was Ella's father. She said he hauled logs out of upper Bluff Creek," Bud remarked as they waited for the dust to settle.

"Could be. The driver was an Indian."

Bud pointed to an opening between two cedar trees at the far edge of the clearing. "That looks like a good campsite." He left the truck and piloted Grammy slowly around rocks and stumps. When she turned off the motor, he asked if she had brought an axe. "If I grub out that big bush, you could park in the shade under the trees."

Grammy stepped out and unlocked a storage compartment. She handed Bud a large axe, and also pulled out a smaller one, a shovel, and a saw. The two worked steadily clearing ground for both the rig and room to sit and cook outdoors. Then Grammy backed in the truck and set the brakes.

"Now, can I make hotcakes?" Bud asked, mopping his face on his shirtsleeve. "I'm so hungry my stomach is stuck to my backbone."

Grammy unlocked the camper door, pulled down the steps, and went inside. She placed the bag of pancake mix, a measuring cup, spoon, and bowl on the counter.

Bud asked for a bigger bowl.

"Bigger? You can make enough batter to serve four people in that one."

Bud explained that as long as he was making hotcakes, he might as well make a lot.

Grammy raised her eyebrows. "Oh. You think Bigfoot might like pancakes? With or without syrup?"

Bud thought a dribble of syrup might help. If bears liked honey, why wouldn't Bigfoot relish syrup on hotcakes?

"Good thinking," Grammy complimented him. She turned her attention to setting the table and peeling oranges.

Bud read the directions on the package of pancake mix. The recipe said a generous individual serving consisted of a stack of four large cakes. He knew he could eat at least two stacks. That would be eight hotcakes, plus four for Grammy, and eight or sixteen more for monster bait. Twenty or twenty-eight hotcakes altogether! Criminy! That was a lot of cooking. Each hotcake had to cook about three to four minutes. The griddle was small, so he could cook only three hotcakes at one time. So, three hotcakes at four minutes' cooking time . . . let's see, he figured . . . three divided into twenty-eight was nine-plus . . . and nine batches of three would consume thirty-six minutes' cooking time . . . over a half hour! Bud gulped. "I guess I'll start with a small batch." He could make more later if Bigfoot developed a big appetite for his cooking.

"Where do you plan to stake out the bait?" Grammy inquired. "Can I help, or do you want to do it on your own?"

As the first batch cooked, Bud looked through the open door to the forest. At this higher elevation the undergrowth was much thinner, and sunlight filtered through the heavy branches. Still, he couldn't see more than a hundred feet, if that far. Also, the tree trunks were large enough for a monster to hide behind. "You can help."

As soon as the first batch cooked, Bud slipped the hotcakes onto plates, and poured a second batch. Both sat down to eat. After a few bites, Grammy said they were cooked to perfection.

"I've had lots of practice." While turning the second batch, Bud thought out loud, gesturing with the spatula. "I was thinking . . . We don't know how long we're going to be here, do we? I like the camper, but it would be more fun to cook outside. I'll clear a fire pit. I know how to make a good one."

Grammy pointed out that in addition to conserving propane fuel, if they cooked outside, their cooking odors would spread further into the forest. If Bigfoot got a good whiff of bacon or hamburger frying, he might . . . investigate.

Bud's eyes sparkled. "Yeah! I've been hoping you'd let me sleep outside, too."

Grammy did not offer a flood of objections. "Of course, you'll want to sleep outside. How else can Bigfoot sneak up in the dark, and kidnap you?"

Bud's jaw sagged until he burst out laughing. Then he mused aloud . . . to save time, or rather to lure Bigfoot sooner, maybe they should stake out the pancake bait right after lunch, before Mr. Ward and his people arrived and started clumping around. Suddenly Bud yawned, but continued thinking aloud. What worried him, he confessed, was that if there were too many people thrashing around the woods, wouldn't they scare off Bigfoot?

Grammy felt that was a possibility. However, Bigfoot was shy. At least, whenever he spied human beings or they spied him, he sped out of sight. Small wonder, considering the number of times he'd been shot at! By now he must have learned that other two-legged creatures were dangerous to him.

Bud's eyes widened. Did his grandmother mean

that if they really, truly wanted to see Bigfoot, they would have to track him on their own? Without all those people tagging along?

Grammy pursed her lips. "Think about it."

Bud thought furiously, as he turned another batch of cakes. True, Bigfoot was shy and wary, but curious! Many times his tracks had been found circling campsites and machinery. Still the few times he had been seen was at dusk, except when Roger Patterson photographed him. Bud reached a decision. "I think we should stake out our bait right after lunch." When Grammy declined another helping, he slid the entire stack on his plate and poured more batter. "We've got to give Mr. Ward a fair try. Then if nothing happens, we should hunt on our own. And if you get too tired, I could hunt on my own." He held his breath, waiting for his grandmother to state flatly that his hunting alone was out of the question. When she said nothing, he exhaled. "I know how to blaze trails so I wouldn't get lost."

By the time he consumed more hotcakes, however, his eyelids were drooping. Grammy suggested that since they had been up since before dawn, why didn't they both take a short nap?

Bud was happy to oblige. He really was too full and too sleepy to go monster hunting right away.

8
• • •

Monster Hair or Moss?

When they wakened, Bud and Grammy laced on hiking boots and Bud buckled a canvas belt around his waist. To this he hooked his sheathed hunting knife and a compass. He also put a small hank of red yarn in his shirt pocket. "Should I carry the tape recorder?"

Grammy didn't think they'd hear Bigfoot whistling or screaming during the heat of the day. She wasn't even going to bother taking her Polaroid camera or binoculars. However, she removed a 30-caliber Winchester rifle and cartridges from a locked compartment at the rear of the closet. "Don't forget the pancakes. They're in the refrigerator, in a sack."

Bud looped the top of the plastic sack through his

belt so his hands would be free. "I'm ready."

Grammy locked the camper and shoved the keys deep into a pocket in her jeans. So Mr. Ward would not worry, she taped a note to the door, stating that she and Bud were on a hike, would blaze their route with red yarn, and return by 4:00 P.M.

Bud led the way, striding across the open ground of the clearing toward the creek. At most it was three yards wide, plunging and gurgling over small boulders in miniature waterfalls. He turned right, upmountain, keeping the creek within sight or hearing. The forest had escaped logging and fires, but the accumulation of centuries of fallen trees and broken limbs made passage a little difficult. The western red cedar and pine trees ranged from four to eight feet in diameter and soared over 150 feet to their crests. They required ample living room, their closely laced branches shutting out some, but not all, of the sunlight. Even at midday a pale golden twilight bathed the tree trunks, deer brush, and huckleberry shrubs. The thick mat of needles and twigs underfoot muffled Bud's footsteps. Every few yards he was forced to circle a huge tree, or climb over a windfall. Soon he called over his shoulder, "I see a game trail."

Even a tenderfoot could have traced the path worn into the matted ground cover. To mark the point where he and Grammy stepped onto the trail,

Bud broke off a piece of yarn and tied it to a bush. Then he turned toward the creek, pausing at the water's edge to search for footprints. When Grammy joined him, he pointed to deer tracks on both banks. "Shall we cross here or stay on this side?" he shouted over the splashing water.

Grammy suggested they consider the creek their west boundary, and explore eastward.

Bud was agreeable. He stripped willow shoots and laid them on the ground, pointing eastward, to mark the direction they were taking. "I'm going to leave a couple of pancakes here." He opened the sack and drew out two, placing one on a rock and the other on an overhanging branch. Then he licked his sticky fingers. "Hey, you did put syrup on them." He swished his hands in the icy water and dried them on his jeans. Again he took the lead, walking slowly and quietly, stopping frequently to look about, and listen, and sniff deeply.

"Blow your nose!" Grammy urged.

Bud explained he was sniffing on purpose, just as a wild animal would do in scenting something strange. "Bigfoot stinks, Grammy. That's what the book said. So, if I smell something bad, I'll know Bigfoot might be close by." He giggled nervously. "I'd rather smell him before he smells me."

The game trail meandered horizontally across the mountainside. As the two moseyed along, Bud did not talk. He knew the sound of human voices carried far, particularly on a quiet windless day. However, woodpeckers and jays telegraphed warnings of their presence. Occasionally Bud heard something snap or thunk nearby, or squirrels skittering up a tree. But there were no heavy noises, the kind an 800-pound monster couldn't help making . . . Bud spun around and peered back along the trail. Whew! Nothing was stalking them.

He draped another pancake over a fallen limb, whispering "First time I ever blazed a trail with pancakes."

A half mile farther both stopped abruptly at the edge of a small meadow. A buck, doe, and twin fawns bounded off into the timber.

"Aw, we scared them," Bud murmured. "We must be making more noise than I thought."

Grammy pointed to small lichen-stained boulders in the clearing. "Let's look around those."

Bud knew porcupines, badgers, and bears overturned rocks searching for fat white grubs. Maybe Bigfoot liked grubs, too. However, after grunting and straining and overturning rock after rock, he found no monster tracks in the grass. He mopped his face on his shirt sleeve. "Guess we might as well move on."

Grammy wanted to investigate the edge of the clearing to see if animals had bedded down there.

Deer sign was abundant, and suddenly she pointed to fresh long scratches on a young tree trunk. "Mountain cat! It's stalking those fawns, or my name isn't Mathilda Miller."

Bud giggled. "Your name is Mathilda Miller, so those have got to be cat tracks." He looked overhead nervously. "I hope it isn't stalking us."

The two poked around the trees and brush until they came to an enormous cedar rent almost its entire length by lightning. The tree lay prostrate, its roots torn from the ground and now suspended like weathered talons over a deep dark cavity. After one glance Bud leaped behind the nearest tree. "That hole looks big enough for a bear's den," he whispered breathlessly.

"Right!"

He peered cautiously from his shelter. "Would Bigfoot sleep in a den like that?"

Grammy chuckled softly. "If you were Bigfoot, would you?"

Bud switched on his imagination. If he were a monster, or even a bear, he sure as shooting would like a roomy, dark, dry shelter like that. Bud stretched his neck and stood on tiptoe to see more of the ground in front of the burrow. He sniffed repeatedly. "Think I dare get closer?" he asked shakily.

"Wait." Grammy slipped a cartridge into the rifle. Then she tiptoed back to the meadow and brought him two small rocks. "Try pitching one into the hole."

Bud's eyes widened. "What if a bear comes out? Or Bigfoot?"

"I'll cover," Grammy said, bracing herself and the rifle against the tree trunk.

Although his heart pounded and his hand trembled, Bud pitched one rock as hard as he could into the opening. Even before he heard it *thunk,* he pulled back against the tree trunk, panting. When a minute passed and no creature rushed out, growling or gnashing its teeth, he relaxed.

"Try again," Grammy whispered, handing him the second rock.

He lobbed this one into the cavern. Again, no protesting beast appeared. Bud was positive the den was empty because, from the sound, the rock obviously had landed on soil, not on an animal's flank. "Gee, I wish I had brought my flashlight. That hole is dark."

"Dark and deep," Grammy whispered.

"I'd like to crawl closer."

Grammy was positive they could do so safely. She could not recall any animals frequenting dark shelters during daylight hours. This late in the year even wild cubs or kits would be out of their dens.

Bud dropped to his hands and knees and inched toward the fallen cedar. He studied the ground in vain for monster or bear tracks. Next he gaped up at the dried exposed roots. He cricked his neck, looking from one to another. Suddenly he grasped his grandmother's arm. His gaze had focused on a small dark mass dangling from one of the roots. He pointed excitedly. "Look at that brown stuff!"

Grammy thought it was probably moss, or fibers of inner bark.

"I bet it's hair! Moss is curly and crinkly." Bud raised to a sprinter's starting position, dashed forward, leaped, and grabbed the dark mass. Then he scuttled away to the far side of another massive tree. When Grammy joined him, he waved his prize under her nose. "See, it *is* hair. It's not moss."

Since they were in the shade, Grammy beckoned Bud to move out into the sunny clearing. Yet even when examined in the brilliant sunlight, it was difficult to judge the exact nature of Bud's discovery. "It's a hank of hair," he kept insisting, poking the brownish-red four-to-six-inch-long tangled strands. They were coarse in texture, but not brittle as dried moss or lichens would have been. Grammy pointed out that the ends of the strands lacked evidence of dried follicles, the saclike tips one would expect to find on hair wrenched from animal or human skin.

"The hair didn't have to be yanked out of Bigfoot's hide," Bud argued. After all, monsters never combed their hair. The longer it grew, the more matted it became. Probably, he thought, when Bigfoot crawled out of that hole, his hair snagged on the sharp roots—a hank pulled free without having follicles or skin attached. "If I had a comb, I bet I could untangle these snarls."

Grammy fingered the strands gently. "I know they're not from a bear. Tell you what. When we get back to the camper, you can examine them under Grampy's magnifying lens. If that doesn't help, show this to Mr. Ward. A biology teacher ought to know whether it's moss or hair."

That pleased Bud. He tucked the hank in his pocket. "Before we leave, I want to put out the last of the pancakes." They returned to the fallen cedar and Bud climbed up on the trunk. He inched along until he could see through the torn roots to the ground. After he secured one of the pancakes on a snag, he asked Grammy below, "Is this high enough so the deer can't eat it?"

Grammy nodded.

"Is it too high? I want Bigfoot to be able to reach it."

Grammy stretched her arms over her head and stood on tiptoe. "Put another one higher."

When the sack was empty, Bud eased back to the ground. He wished there was some way of keeping birds or squirrels from eating the pancakes before Bigfoot found them. "Do you think they'll be eaten by tomorrow?"

Tomorrow or the next day, Grammy guessed. The only way he could find out would be to return to the places where he had staked out the bait.

Bud wished he could return alone to the uprooted cedar. He liked having his grandmother along, and didn't want to hurt her feelings. Still, there were some things a fellow needed to do on his own, without a grownup telling him what to do. Chances were Grammy wouldn't allow him to venture into the forest alone this soon. His mother surely wouldn't, if she were here. She'd line out enough objections to program a computer. But maybe it wouldn't hurt to ask. If Grammy said no, he could keep pestering until she gave in. "Could I come back here by myself? I mean, you don't have to come if you don't want to. I wouldn't get lost. Honest."

Grammy took her time answering. If he felt he must return alone, and promised to stay on the trail and go no farther than the clearing, he could.

Bud whooped joyfully. "Can I bring a flashlight and look down in the hole?"

"Don't know why not," she answered calmly.

"What if Bigfoot has made a bed in there?"

"Then you'd want a picture, wouldn't you? You'd probably need the flash attachment on the camera."

"R-i-g-h-t." Bud answered slowly, his mind churning with exciting ideas. First, he'd sneak up on the opening, and probe the depths with the flashlight.

But suppose Bigfoot was hiding in there? Or sleeping? How could he use the flashlight and take a picture at the same time? If he spied Bigfoot, and Bigfoot spied him, he'd have to snap the photograph and depend on the light from the flash cube blinding the monster momentarily so he could skedaddle away. Otherwise, Bigfoot might reach out with a l-o-n-g arm or hairy paw . . . no, hand . . . and grab him! "Yeah," Bud gasped, his voice quavering, "I sure will need the flash attachment."

Grammy nodded. "Say, wasn't it Kit Carson who escaped a grizzly's charge by hurling gravel in its eyes? Or was that Jim Bridger? Maybe you better keep that in mind."

Bud concentrated on his hands. If he held the flashlight in his left hand . . . and the camera in the right hand . . . how could he scoop up dirt and throw it, if he had to all of a sudden? He made a few practice gestures.

Grammy tapped him on the shoulder. "We better move on. See how the sun's rays are slanting through the trees? Mr. Ward might be wondering where we are."

Bud switched his thinking to more practical matters. "Shouldn't we stay here until dark? Bigfoot might show up, and we'd miss him."

Grammy didn't feel that staying until dark would be wise. First, it would be unfair to worry Mr. Ward and the others, who hadn't the slightest idea where they were. Secondly, they should get to know the immediate area better so, if they had to, they could move about without becoming lost. Besides, wasn't he anxious to show Mr. Ward the monster hair?

Bud immediately swallowed his objections to leaving. "Okay, let's go."

9

• • •

Sitting in the Dark Is Dumb

Again Bud led the way along the game trail until it dipped down to the logging road. Then he walked on one side, Grammy on the other, searching for monster tracks. However, the moment he smelled wood smoke and heard voices, he broke into a fast trot. The campsite seemed crowded, now that the other members of the expedition had arrived. When Bud spied the leader pounding tent stakes into the ground, he raced to his side. "Mr. Ward! Look't what I found! Bigfoot hair!"

Mr. Ward examined the tangled mass intently. He turned the almost weightless bulk over and over, pulled a strand through his fingers, smelled it, even unraveled a strand and chewed on it. Bud almost exploded with suspense before being asked, "Where did you find this?"

Bud babbled, "Snagged on a root. See, this big cedar tree had been struck by lightning, and all the roots were pulled out, and—"

"Exactly where?" the teacher interrupted. "Along the road? In the woods? How far from here?"

Bud took a deep breath before describing the route he and Grammy had taken up the creek to the game trail, east along the trail to the clearing, and around the clearing to the fallen cedar. "You can't miss it. I blazed the trail. That's hair I found, isn't it? My grandmother knows a lot about bears. She says it isn't from a bear."

Instead of answering, Mr. Ward called to a young man named Jim Finch. "Jim, step over here a minute." He handed the strands to Jim to examine. "What have we got—hair, fur, or moss?"

Jim rubbed the strands so roughly between his thumb and fingers that Bud winced. "Hey, take it easy. That's important evidence."

"Where'd you find it?"

Bud launched into another long explanation. Jim gave the material back to Mr. Ward. "It's moss."

"It is not!" Bud exclaimed, stamping his foot. "It's Bigfoot hair!" He was so upset he nearly burst into tears. He looked around frantically. "Grammy, come here." With his attention diverted, he missed seeing Jim flick a glance at the specimen and silently mouth a word to Ward.

As Grammy walked up, Bud complained, "Mr. Finch says this stuff is only moss."

Grammy put her arm across Bud's shoulders. "Calm down, Bud. Give Mr. Ward a chance to explain."

The leader smiled. "Sorry to upset your grandson, Mrs. Miller. Jim and I are positive this is only moss. However, I'd like to keep it for further study. I can have it, can't I, Bud?"

Bud's face flushed. "No! If it's only moss, how come you want it?"

The reason was that Mr. Ward planned to gather many specimens to help demonstrate to his students the nature of the forest growth in Bigfoot country.

"I collect stuff, too," Bud informed him, holding out his hand.

"Well, in that case—" He placed the moss in Bud's hand.

An awkward silence followed. Grammy asked hastily if an organized search for Bigfoot was scheduled later in the day.

There certainly was, Mr. Ward assured her. He had assigned one pickup to transport half the expedition members three miles down the road for their monster watch. A second pickup would patrol the twisting dirt road between the campsite and the logging operation farther on up the mountain. Both vehicles would leave promptly at six-thirty, and if nothing exciting occurred, would return not later than midnight.

"You can count on our reporting to your tent promptly at six-thirty," Grammy said. With a firm hand she turned Bud toward the camper.

Bud grumbled every step of the way. If his find was not monster hair, why did Mr. Ward want to keep it? If he kept it, he wouldn't tell people Bud had found it. He'd take all the credit for himself. He was jealous, that's what. He wasn't going to give a mere kid credit for finding something important. He—

"Shush!" Grammy ordered as she unlocked the camper. "I don't want to hear any more talk like that. We're going to have a glass of orange juice, and study the moss or hair under Grampy's magnifying glass."

The cool drink made Bud feel better, but the magnifying glass did not. He peered through it until his eyes watered but still did not learn anything more about the true nature of the brownish-red strands. Then he tried to comb them but could not untangle the snarls. "Now what?" he said grumpily.

"Now we are going to stop pouting, and build a fire pit. Then we'll cook hamburgers, and afterwards, report for the evening search. And you, young man, will behave. I was mortified at the way you talked to Mr. Ward."

Bud sulked. "I'm not going to ride in the same truck with him."

While Grammy unlaced her hiking boots and slipped on moccasins, she reminded Bud again they were members of an expedition. Therefore, until they chose to be on their own, they would cooperate with the leader.

Bud stuck out his jaw. "I'm still going back to that cedar tree alone tomorrow morning."

"Shape up, or you won't be going anywhere on your own." Grammy's tone of voice was calm, as usual, but left no doubt in Bud's mind. She would tolerate no more childishness.

Bud hustled outside and set to work building a proper fire pit and laying the fire. Grammy assembled a portable metal table and camp stools, then went inside to prepare the salad greens and hamburger patties.

When the fire was blazing and the grate in place, Bud talked to her through the open window. He wondered if his air mattress and sleeping bag would be safe if he arranged his bed before they left later on. He would rather blow up the mattress now, before dinner. He couldn't blow hard when his stomach was full.

Grammy felt certain their campsite would not be

molested. After he fixed his bed, he could haul a bucket of water from the creek. Kool-Aid tasted much better made with fresh cold creek water. Then he could attach the flash attachment to the camera, and lay out the other articles he planned to take on his early morning hike.

Bud strained on tiptoe to whisper, "If I see Bigfoot tomorrow, I'm not going to say one word to Mr. Ward."

Grammy chortled. "You'll tell me, I hope."

"Only if you promise not to tell Mr. Ward."

It was too soon for promises like that. Furthermore, Grammy warned, he was to stop thinking bad thoughts about Mr. Ward. "If you tried, you might like him."

Bud gagged noisily. "Yech!" He turned away to finish his chores.

At 6:25 Grammy switched on the camper outdoor light, and locked the door. Then she and Bud reported to the leader's tent. Mr. Ward had nailed a bulletin board to a tree. On it was a list of every member's name, and the pickup truck each was assigned to for the evening patrol. Mr. Ward stressed how important it was that each cross his or her name off the list before going to bed, so he would know everyone was back in camp. He repeated instructions given earlier. "Never, never leave camp without signing out. Note the approximate area or direction you expect to visit. Then go *there,* not somewhere else. If you should get lost or have an accident, heaven forbid, we'll have a better chance of locating you." After everyone nodded, he called out the names of those assigned to Pickup Number One and Pickup Number Two. "Number One patrols up-mountain, Number Two down-mountain. Any questions? No? All right, let's go."

Instead of racing to be first to climb into the back of Pickup Number One, Bud dragged his feet.

"What's the matter now?" Grammy whispered.

"I told you, I'm not going in the same truck as Mr. Ward."

"His name was not on the list of those riding Number One," she hissed impatiently. "Come on!"

"His name wasn't on the list for Number Two, either. If he isn't riding on One or Two, where is he going to hunt?"

Grammy shook a finger under Bud's nose. "Are you going to ride with me, or stay here by yourself and suck your thumb?"

Since the last thing Bud wanted was to be left behind, he helped Grammy climb up onto the truck bed. The driver was Mr. Neilson. He and his wife were so fat no one could share the seat inside the cab with them. "Are you ready?" he sang out. When everyone shouted, he raced the motor, ground the gears, and roared off in a cloud of dust.

Meanwhile the forest scene three miles beyond the camp had changed at 4:00 P.M., when the logging operation shut down. The last logging truck churned out of the loading yard. The high screech of the power-driven saw ceased. Bulldozer and loading crane motors ground to a stop, and the steel cables strung a thousand feet or more from the top of the spar pole out to felled trees went limp. After the pickup transporting the crew downmountain to their camp withdrew, a healing quiet mantled the forest. As the dust settled, large bold black and blue Steller's jays and gray Clark's nutcrackers swooped down to feed on lunch pail leavings and insects exposed by the logging. A badger, then chipmunks and smaller birds, gradually ventured forth, and lastly the deer. When the sun dipped below the crest of the high ridges on the west, soft violet-blue shadows deepened.

Suddenly a nutcracker sounded an alarm with his flat, grating call, *khaa-khaa*. Even before the harsh notes died out, the clearing was deserted. Not long after, three men stumbled wearily from a trail onto the deeply rutted road. They were unshaven, their shirts and jeans caked with dirt, their shoulders humped under the weight of backpacks and rifles. They slogged on down the road. A mile further one said, "Truck coming." As Mr. Neilson's pickup ground to a stop alongside them, one of the young men riding in it greeted the strangers. "How's fishing?"

"Lousy," all agreed.

"We're hunting for Bigfoot," Bud informed them. "You didn't happen to see him, did you?"

"No, worse luck," the oldest of the three newcomers answered. "See you." They waved and moved on.

Mr. Neilson ground the gears and continued on up the road. His passengers speculated about who the strangers could be and guessed they must be the owners of the camper and tent set up by the creek at the expedition headquarters.

Shortly after, Mr. Neilson drove into the logging site and parked alongside a huge yellow diesel-powered loading machine mounted on crawler treads. In comparison the pickup looked like a toy truck. As the passengers jumped to the ground, he stepped out of the cab and yodeled loudly.

"Shhhhh!" several admonished him nervously. "We're supposed to be quiet."

Bud's lips curled, and he whispered disgustedly to Grammy, "Him, Tarzan."

Mr. Neilson's feelings were hurt. He not only prided himself on his yodeling, he was certain that if Bigfoot were near, the beast would answer the call. However, if Bigfoot heard him, he did not respond.

98

The monster hunters poked around gingerly, searching the ground around the logging landing, or work area, for Bigfoot tracks. Later they walked quietly a short distance through an opening cleared by a bulldozer to the place where the trees were felled. Perhaps because the light was fading and the thickets blurred by shadows, all stayed within a few yards of each other. Everywhere the ground was littered with chunks of thick bark and broken branches, and deeply scoured by the bulldozer's lugs. There were also many tracks in the powdery dust. To everyone's disappointment they were those of loggers' boots and deer, not of a huge five-toed monster.

After the logging landing had been scrutinized, Bud and two others picked up branches and broomed the ground around the machinery free of tracks. Mr. Ward had told them Bigfoot was very curious about machinery. At least his footprints had been discovered frequently circling machinery. Mr. Neilson thought sweeping the ground was a waste of time. Even if Bigfoot passed by after they all left, the loggers would rub out his tracks in the morning.

Grammy wondered aloud if someone could drive up before the loggers started to work, and check the ground before it was disturbed.

No one volunteered to venture out before sunrise, when logging operations commenced.

Bud tugged on Grammy's sleeve. She waited until

there was enough distance between her and the others so Bud could talk without being overheard. "This is a neat place to hunt for Bigfoot. Look at all the machinery, and soft dirt. Let's come up before sunrise and hunt on our own for his footprints."

Grammy shrugged. "All right, but I thought you wanted to hike back to the uprooted cedar tree."

"I did . . . do. I mean, I could do that after we came up here."

Grammy wondered why Bud thought the logging area would be any more interesting to Bigfoot than their campground. There he would have more people to spy on, and pickup trucks, clothes strung on lines, coolers with food in them, and motorcycles. The garbage pit might attract him, too.

Bud's eyebrows arched, and he giggled. "Yeah, motorcycles! Boy, would I love to see Bigfoot on a motorcycle."

Cooking odors should attract him, too, Grammy pointed out.

"But maybe there're too many people at the campsite."

"Maybe there're too many people right here," Grammy answered. "I still can't see hunting in crowds. Wild creatures avoid crowds. When Grampy stalked grizzlies in Alaska, he never went out with more than one guide and me. Tell you what. Let's see what Mr. Ward lines out for us in the next day or two. If we think we're wasting our time, we'll make other plans. Okay?"

Bud was satisfied.

A close examination of the area where the trees were being logged off yielded no sign of Bigfoot. Three of the young people volunteered to keep watch there for an hour or two. The others returned to the pickup and climbed in back. They sat and sat, and waited and waited, but no huge dark manlike hairy creature emerged from the forest. About nine o'clock Mr. Neilson started the motor, quietly this time, and drove slowly without lights on down the mountain to the campsite. It appeared to be deserted. He made a U-turn and drove back one mile, and parked. After twenty minutes he moved on a half mile and parked; another half mile and parked; finally, he returned to the yarding area. The three young people blinked a flashlight briefly, and climbed into the truck bed.

"See anything?" Bud asked hopefully.

"Nothing."

The monster watchers were stiff from sitting on the metal truck bed, sleepy, and bored by the time Mr. Neilson announced, "Eleven o'clock. Let's go." When no one objected, he returned to the campsite and parked alongside his camper. His passengers dropped to the ground, mumbled thanks, and moved off to their sleeping quarters.

"Hey, everybody forgot to scratch names off the list," Bud remembered as he and Grammy walked past Mr. Ward's tent. The leader had considerately left a small lantern burning by the bulletin board. Bud used the pencil tied to a string to scratch the names of all who had returned in Pickup Number One.

Back in their camper Bud undressed first, gave his grandmother a peck on the cheek, and mumbled, "G'night. See you in the morning." He opened the door, but then turned to say, "I think sitting in the dark is dumb, dumb, dumb." Then he closed the door behind him and walked to his sleeping bag. As soon as he was settled and the zipper drawn up to his chin, he called out, "You can turn off the light now."

Grammy switched off the outdoor light. But a few seconds later she asked through an open window, "You're sure you'll be all right?"

"Yeah. I'm fine. I put my boots inside my sleeping bag."

"Have you got a can of snuff?"

"Snuff? What would I need a can of snuff for?" Then he remembered, and chortled, "Hunh-uh. I don't think Bigfoot'll kidnap me tonight." He yawned, and fell asleep with a smile on his face.

10

• • •

"Hey, Bigfoot! Come on Out!"

When Bud wakened at first light, he opened his eyes very slowly. He hadn't been kidnapped, but he wanted to be very sure Bigfoot wasn't prowling around the campsite. Raising his head slightly, he looked about but spied nothing suspicious. Just in case the creature was lurking in the woods close by, Bud opened the sleeping bag zipper quickly, jammed on his boots, and dashed toward the camper.

The moment the door handle squeaked, Grammy opened one eye, saw Bud entering, and pretended to be asleep. Bud took great pains not to disturb her, in case she had second thoughts about his venturing out alone. He dressed quickly, pulling on a sweat-shirt because the air was cool. After lacing on his

103

boots, he snapped the flashlight to his belt, picked up the camera, and quietly closed the camper door behind him.

As anxious as Bud was to reach the fallen cedar, he took time to check on the pancakes he had left by the creek. They had not been disturbed, nor were there any unusual footprints at the water's edge. He turned and strode eastward, scarcely glancing at the pancakes he had left along the trail. He was grateful for the strand of bright red yarn which marked the point where they had entered the clearing the previous afternoon. There were no deer feeding in the meadow. He moved with extreme caution under cover of the trees, from trunk to trunk around the perimeter of the clearing. Finally he spied the fallen cedar. Crouching low, he moved closer until he had an unobstructed view of the exposed roots and the dark cavity beneath them.

He froze into position until certain he had identified the noises roundabout: uppermost limbs of the tall cedars and pines rubbing softly, a dead branch plummeting to the ground, the soft whoosh of an owl winging by. Not until his heartbeat slowed did he wipe one hand and then the other on his jeans, check the camera setting, and prepare to take his first photograph.

The evening before, while sitting in the dark on the uncomfortable truck bed, he had thought out

104

what to do. Somehow peering into the hole and flashing the flashlight in a monster's or a bear's face had little appeal. He really didn't want to come face to face with Bigfoot *that* way. Then he realized he wouldn't need the flashlight to probe the depths. If he crept up on the opening, he could extend the camera over the edge. Quickly—one, two, three—he could point it downward, trigger the lens and flash, and streak behind the nearest big tree. Meanwhile the camera would develop the film. When the process was completed, Bud would know whether the dark hole was inhabited or not. If Bigfoot or a bear emerged blinking, he would be long gone down the trail before either regained its sight.

The moment Bud triggered the flash, he darted off to the left. Since the camera was an older model Polaroid, he had to count the seconds that must elapse before he pulled the exposed film from the camera. At the same time he watched tensely to see if a monster or bear, or even a skunk, emerged from the hole. When none stumbled from the depths, he exhaled noisily. "Whew!"

His hand shook as he peeled the photograph from its cover. "Wow, wow, WOW!" he gloated. He had a detailed picture of three sides and the bottom of the cavity.

It was empty.

Since he was in deep shade, he stepped to the edge

of the clearing, and parted branches to gain better light. When he looked again at the picture, he had to grit his teeth to keep from whooping at the top of his lungs. There was a bed of sorts at the bottom of the hole! Some creature—two-legged or four-legged—had brought in small branches, clumps of moss and some fibrous material, and leaves. The leaves were withered. That meant the bed had not been made recently.

Bud's heart pounded so, he gasped for breath. Moments passed before he dared move. When he returned to the hole, he took greater care in aiming the camera and snapped another exposure. Again he withdrew to the edge of the clearing, counting off the seconds. "Aw, shucks," he muttered when he viewed the second photograph. He was disappointed because it revealed no finger marks, no claw scratches, no tracks or footprints. Boldly now, he strode back to the hole and knelt at the edge. His first thought was to crawl down inside and examine the interior closely with the flashlight. Then he rejected the idea. He was leery of rattlesnakes. Also he must not disturb the interior, especially not contaminate it with his man-scent. Otherwise, whatever creature frequented the den would avoid using it until the last trace of his foreign scent faded out. He had already promised himself he would return morning after morning until he saw, or positively identified, the occupant.

106

Back on his feet, he gazed upward through the branches. The pancakes had not been eaten. Next he climbed on the fallen trunk and photographed the ground below. Again he was disappointed. Filming from that elevated position did not expose any heavy imprints on the tough slippery carpet of needles and twigs. Perhaps it was because the ground was so dry. Even his own tracks did not show. Or, he guessed after more thought, maybe the tracks were there but didn't show because of the dim, before-sunrise light. Maybe if he waited until the sun had risen, he could see more. Sometimes really important bits of evidence were overlooked because of the angle from which they were viewed. At least, that's what he'd learned watching his favorite television detective.

"Ye-ah," he murmured, firing up his imagination. He'd act like a real detective. Yesterday, if he hadn't cricked his neck until it hurt, and squinted at every single exposed root, he'd never have found the hank of hair.

Fingers trembling with excitement, Bud placed his photographs side by side on the tree trunk, and studied them intently. Did they contain a clue he had missed? Hmmm . . . Suddenly he jabbed a finger at something revealed in the bottom of the den. Moss! Strips of moss, crinkly, splotchcd, gray-whitc-green-black. Not brownish-red. Not in tangled strands. Where had that moss come from?

He looked about. The standing tree trunks were

daubed with moss, and the windfalls and rotten branches heavily encrusted with both moss and lichens. He turned on his buttocks and peered the length of the fallen cedar. There were no places where patches of moss had been scraped off. He stood up and, with feet apart for better balance, examined at eye level the trunks of the trees nearest him. Nothing there . . . nor there . . . He raised his head and looked about at a higher level, ten to twelve feet above the ground. Nothing torn from that tree, nor that one . . . there! . . . to the right of the den! . . . not only a large strip of moss was missing, but a huge slab of the foot-thick outer bark had been wrenched loose, exposing the fibrous inner material.

"O-h, criminy, this poor light!" Bud couldn't see if there were claw scratches on the trunk. Maybe they would show up on film. He peered through the view finder, sharpened the focus, and triggered the shutter and flash. The exposed film revealed nary a claw mark.

"Yahoo!" Bud hollered, unable to quench his joy. The absence of claw marks convinced him that Bigfoot had gathered the moss. He scrambled to the ground and ran to the foot of the tree, thoughtlessly tramping on the short already-mangled brush at its base. A large slab of bark lay on the ground, its inner fibers torn free, while another section had been partially loosened from the trunk. Bud braced one foot against the tree and pulled hard on the bark. He could not loosen it. When he looked upward, he realized only a very tall creature could pull down moss from such a height. That creature just had to be Bigfoot!

Anxious to see the moss at close hand, Bud stepped around the trunk until he found a patch within reach. Clutching a fistful, he almost danced to the edge of the clearing. The moss, or lichens, were not brownish-red, and had none of the appearance of hair. Once more Bud whooped at the top of his lungs. This time he did hear sounds from close by, but they faded into the distance. He must have startled the deer. Undoubtedly the crackling he heard was from their bounding off into the forest. Exuberantly Bud added his own happy stomping, like an Indian dancing a victory celebration.

Certain now that he had found a monster's hideaway, Bud sought more evidence. He walked about slowly, head down, knees bent. If only the light were better! When he found nothing, he got down on his hands and knees, and crawled about the trunks of the nearest trees. Suddenly he did spy something white and small almost hidden under a shrub. He picked it up.

"A cigarette stub!"

The blood throbbed in his veins. The paper on the butt was still white. It had not yellowed from exposure yet, nor been ground under a boot heel. It had been flicked away, obviously still burning, because there were a few charred needles where it had lain. Bud's mind roiled with suspicions. Mr. Ward had done this. Mr. Ward was the only one, other than Grammy, who knew about this place. Instead of hunting with the others last evening, he had sneaked off to find a hank of Bigfoot's hair for himself. The moment he had seen Bud's prize, he had realized its value. That's why he had Bud tell him *exactly* where it had been found. Bud's chest swelled with the satisfaction of knowing he had been right. He had found something tremendously important, and Mr. Ward wanted a specimen for himself so he could take the credit for finding it.

"Ye-ah," Bud agreed with himself. He was more positive than ever that Mr. Ward could not be trusted. He was sneaky . . . and jealous . . . and—he didn't smoke.

Bud squirmed as he remembered this. No, Mr. Ward did not smoke. What's more, he warned everyone repeatedly to be extremely careful with matches and cigarettes while in the woods. Every teacher Bud ever had worked hard to convince students of the necessity for protecting wildlife and the land, and how to prevent pollution and forest fires. So Mr. Ward would never be the one to carelessly cause a forest fire. But someone had flipped that cigarette

110

under the bush only a few hours ago. Who? Jim Finch? Bud rapped his knuckles on his head. He couldn't remember whether he had seen Mr. Finch smoking or not. But he knew about this place, too!

Bud tucked the cigarette stub in his shirt pocket. It shouldn't be hard to prove that Mr. Finch smoked this particular brand. The thought made Bud's eyes sparkle. He rapped his knuckles on his head again. "Hey, Miller, use the ol' bean. Make like a detective on television." Where should he begin? Maybe he should hide under a shrub and wait for someone or some *thing* to approach the den. When he—or it—appeared, Bud would take a picture. For evidence. Ye-ah, for in-con-tro-vertible evidence. That's what detectives needed . . . in-con-tro-vertible stuff. But suppose Bigfoot or Mr. Finch or Mr. Ward didn't show up until dark. Grammy would worry and come looking for him. Besides, he was hungry. It would be better to return to the camper now.

Chortling, jubilant, Bud worked his way back to the game trail and headed west. Part way back he paused to look around. The sun had risen, banishing the gloom and heavy shadows. The reddish cedar and yellow pine trunks glowed softly in the shimmering filtered light. Foraging birds and squirrels socialized overhead in the branches. Bud called to them, and laughed when they chirped in reply. Impulsively he cupped his hands around his mouth and shouted, "Hey, Bigfoot! Come on out! . . . You hear me, Bigfoot? Come on out!"

After a long wait, Bud jogged on happily to the camper. Had he been less excited, had he taken the time to return to the creek, he would have discovered that the pancakes had been eaten, and deep tracks in the gravelly creek bed were being washed out by the swift, tumbling water.

11

• • •

Bigfoot's Lair

When Bud entered the camper his grandmother was sitting at the table in her pajamas, drinking coffee. "Glad you're back safe and sound. Did you get any good pictures?"

"Did I?" Bud bragged. "Look here!" He sat down and carefully placed his photographs in one-two-three-four order before her. "See anything special?"

As Grammy studied the prints, her eyes widened. "Boughs . . . and moss! In that hole! I can't believe my eyes."

Bud bounced excitedly on the cushion, laughing in happy bursts. "Yeah! Isn't that great? I could hardly wait to show you."

Grammy studied the pictures further. Then she

113

eyed Bud. "You didn't put that stuff in there just to fool your old grandmother?"

Bud crossed his heart. "No, no! I didn't climb down in there, or toss stuff in. I didn't want to contaminate anything with my scent." He bounced more. "Grammy, that's got to be Bigfoot's lair! A bear wouldn't drag in boughs and moss, would it?"

Grammy didn't think so, though she could be wrong. Coyotes sometimes lined a den with a little grass. However, none of the dens used by bears while hibernating, which she had seen, contained bedding material. She picked up the magnifying glass and examined the prints again. "Usually a bear's den has lots of hair in it—top, sides, and bottom, because bears squirm in their sleep, and scratch. One way of identifying a coyote's or wolf's lair from a bear's is by the hair found in it."

Bud leaned back. "What about a mountain lion? We saw where one had clawed a tree, remember?"

Grammy confessed she didn't know.

"I found where Bigfoot scraped strips of moss from a tree. There weren't any claw marks on the tree trunk, so it had to be Bigfoot that did it."

"Sometimes claw marks on deeply furrowed bark are hard to see," she cautioned. Bud mustn't jump to any false conclusions.

Bud showed her moss from the tree trunk so she could compare it with the fragments seen in the photograph. "It's the same. It isn't anywhere near like

114

that hank of hair I found." He laid the moss and hank side by side. "See?"

Grammy saw. "You've turned up a real mystery. Oh, if only Grampy were here. He could tell at a glance what you found." She sighed, but then smiled at Bud. "Well, sir, you've had a very fruitful morning."

Bud giggled. "That's not all I found. Now, look at this." With a great flourish he displayed the cigarette stub. "Was I ever mad when I saw this, and some scorched pine needles under it. Now I know why Mr. Ward's name wasn't on the lists of those riding the pickups last night. I bet he and that Jim Finch went to my tree to find some more Bigfoot hair!"

After examining the stub, Grammy leaned back. "You didn't see any man-sized boot marks there?"

"Hunh-uh, and I sure looked. Y'know what I think? I think Mr. Ward recognized right away I found something special, and couldn't wait to see that hole for himself." Bud snapped his fingers. "Hey, could Mr. Ward have put that stuff in the bottom of the hole, just to trick me?"

Mr. Ward was not that kind of person, Grammy stated firmly. "Look, we could talk all day and know nothing more than we are guessing right now. What say we cook breakfast?" She slipped off her seat cushion. "Anything special you'd like?"

"Just more pancakes. I'll fix 'em."

When Bud went outside to start the fire, he noticed several other fires blazing around the campsite. Mr. Ward and Jim Finch were standing by one, talking and sipping coffee. Other expedition members were chopping wood or cooking. A stranger, a tall thin white-haired man, came from the creek with a bucket of water in one hand, a fishing rod in the other. A younger man stepped down from a camper, and then the two talked with a third man whom Bud could see preparing a meal inside the camper. Bud recognized them as the ones seen on the road the previous evening.

After breakfast Bud walked over to read the bulletin board alongside Mr. Ward's tent. The teacher spoke to him, but not Jim Finch. Since Mr. Finch wasn't smoking, Bud couldn't play detective. He thought about asking him what brand of cigarettes he smoked, but decided not to. Mr. Finch probably would call him a nosey kid. Besides, Bud told himself, a question like that might reveal that Bud had made an early morning trip to the fallen cedar. He checked the day's assignments, groaned, and hustled back to the camper. "Guess what? We're teamed with the Neilsons. Can't we tell Mr. Ward right now we'd rather be on our own?"

Grammy shook her head and told Bud to go tell the Neilsons they would be ready to leave any time. Bud scuffed through the dust and back. "They haven't even had breakfast. Criminy! The morning will be gone before they're ready to leave."

Grammy chuckled. "You can spend the time chopping firewood. I'll nip inside and fix a meatloaf and dessert for dinner."

About a half hour later the white-haired stranger walked over to their campsite. "Morning," he addressed Bud. "My friends and I have run out of coffee. How're the chances to borrow some?"

Bud pointed to the window over the sink in the camper. "You'll have to ask my grandmother."

The stranger was so tall he could look through the screen at Grammy. "Morning, ma'am. I'm Tom Eads." He pointed toward his outfit. "The boys and I are out of coffee. Any chance of borrowing a little? We'll be driving down to the store at Weitchpec tomorrow, and can replace it then."

Grammy slid the screen to one side. "You bet. How about a cup right now?" She handed Eads a mug. "I'm Matty Miller from San Diego. You spoke to my grandson, Bud. We've been wondering who our missing neighbors were. Have a seat. I'll be right out." She filled a small plastic sack with coffee from a container for the visitor, poured herself a cup of coffee, and stepped outside. Mr. Eads waited until she perched on a camp stool before seating himself. Bud sat on the ground, facing them. "Any luck fishing?"

Eads took two long swallows of coffee before speaking. "Good coffee! No, no luck fishing. Creek's too shallow. The boys are going to hike down to Bluff Creek later on and see if they can raise some. How about you? Did you come up to fish?"

Grammy explained that she and Bud were part of the Ward expedition.

"I wondered why so many rigs were here. Usually we have this place pretty much to ourselves." He smiled. "You're not loggers, and you're not fishing. So you must be hunting Bigfoot."

"Right."

"Any luck?" Eads asked quickly.

Bud opened his mouth, but Grammy cut in, "Not so far."

Eads looked from one to the other. "You were in that truck driving up to the logging landing last evening?"

"Yes. How come you were on the road last night?"

Eads guessed he'd better explain. He was a professional wildlife photographer. He and his companions had just peeled off the mountainside from a three-week trek through the timber.

"Did you get a picture of Bigfoot?" Bud interrupted.

Not a one, the man admitted.

"Was this your first trip?"

"Hardly!" Tom Eads claimed he was an old-timer

at monster hunting. This was his seventh trip to Bluff Creek.

Bud's jaw sagged. "Your seventh? And you've never seen Bigfoot?"

Grammy told the photographer, "Bud expected to have Bigfoot all tied up in blue ribbon within a few days after starting to hunt for him. I keep telling him some people have hunted year after year without success, but I don't think he believes me."

"Your grandmother is right," Eads told Bud. "Maybe I shouldn't say this, but I will anyway. You're never going to see him tagging along with a crowd. You're wasting your time."

Bud clapped his hands. "That's what I've been telling Grammy. We wouldn't be here this late in the morning, only we have to wait for Mr. and Mrs. Neilson to have breakfast. We should be hunting on our own. Grammy and I are good hikers. We know our way around the mountains." He giggled. "Grammy's part mountain goat."

Grammy quipped, "And you're part mountain *kid!*"

"I guessed as much," Eads admitted. "You may have a brand-new rig, but your camping gear has that well-used look." He pointed to the portable table made of metal rods encased in a worn canvas case. "I haven't seen a table like that in forty years."

Grammy was pleased. "That old table has been

set up in every mining camp in the West and Alaska. My husband was a mining engineer. He had that table and long-handled skillet from his university days."

"And now you're hunting Bigfoot. Well! Tell me, why do you want to find him? What will you do if you succeed?"

Bud made a face. "Gee, no one ever asked us that."

"Then it's time we thought out the answers, isn't it?" Grammy replied. "I guess we're just curious."

"Re-al curious," Bud emphasized. "We won't know whether this monster business is a hoax until we see him with our own eyes."

Eads repeated a question. What would they do if they succeeded?

Grandmother and grandson exchanged glances. Then Bud burbled, "Take a picture of him!"

"You don't plan to shoot him?"

Both were horrified. "No!" Grammy added that she carried a rifle much of the time as protection against bears. "But I would never shoot a rare creature like Bigfoot . . . assuming there is a Bigfoot."

Bud remarked, "Mr. Ward would shoot him, I bet, and Jim Finch, too. Else why did they bring guns along?"

"For the same reason I did," Grammy replied.

Tom Eads shook his head. "I'd like to think you were right, dear lady, but I've seen too many hunters the past seven years. They prattle a lot about protecting the creature. Nonsense! They're all out to capture or kill one in order to get a lot of publicity, and make a lot of money. We can be thankful none have succeeded so far."

Bud was puzzled. With so many hunting Bigfoot, why hadn't anyone succeeded?

Mostly because they were Sunday-hunters, Eads felt, more a threat to themselves than Bigfoot. Even the few professionals with trained dogs failed. "Once you set foot in these mountains, you're in Bigfoot's country. It's his territory. He has all the advantages. How well I know! He's led me a merry chase."

Bud said he wouldn't want to see Bigfoot killed, or caged in a zoo. However, until some one did capture him, how would people really learn about him?

"Mostly through photography," Eads remarked. "The boys and I—one is my son, Jack, the other a graduate student in animal behavior—hope to locate an area frequented by the creature and its family. Then we'll construct a blind, or shelter, from which to observe the creatures without their seeing us, and photograph them over a short period, possibly a week or two, maybe more. That's what we hoped to do this last trip, but failed." He realized biologists would want much more information than a photographer could offer, "but just proving Bigfoot exists would satisfy me." Then he laughed. "Of course, I'd

121

make money selling photographs. Photography is a career for me, and my equipment has cost me thousands of dollars. I'd appreciate some return on my investment. But at least I wouldn't have the creature's injury or death on my conscience."

Now Grammy had a question. "You used the word *family*. You think there's more than one creature?"

There had to be a family unit, and more than one family, Eads averred. For over one hundred years females and young ones, in addition to adult males, had been observed all the way from British Columbia to northern California. "The one Roger Patterson photographed near here was a female. I've talked with old Hoopa and Yurok Indians who claim to have seen family groups. One man I know who hunts Bigfoot the year around insists there could be as many as two hundred family groups in the Pacific Northwest."

Bud shivered. "Wow! What does this man think Bigfoot is . . . a human or an animal?"

"We both figure he's a subhuman species which somehow has survived for thousands of years."

Grammy remarked sympathetically, "What a pity you couldn't find him. Didn't you see anything on this trip?"

"Lots of footprints."

"Near here?" Bud interrupted.

Eads touched the ground. "Not here, but as close as the logging area up the mountain."

"You mean, where we were walking around last night, in the dark?" He kicked his heels together. "Wow! Bigfoot could have been spying on us!" He smacked the palm of one hand on his forehead. "And I thought sitting in the truck was dumb. Wait till we tell the others what you said."

"Don't tell them," Eads pleaded sharply. "The word would spread, and this place would be swarming with Sunday-hunters. Our chances of seeing him close by would be ruined."

"We won't tell," Bud promised. He moved on his buttocks closer to Eads and lowered his voice. "Did you see any other signs?"

The photographer nodded, saying he had brought back something that remembled a hank of the creature's hair.

"Hair!" Bud whooped.

"Shhh!" Grammy asked Eads to tell them more about the hair.

There wasn't much to tell. Phil, the graduate student, claimed it was unlike anything he had ever studied under a microscope. Eads had seen similar hair, or whatever it was, plucked from shrubs in Ape Canyon on the slope of Mount St. Helens in southwestern Washington, and from a rock shelter discovered in the mountains northwest of Harrison Lake in British Columbia. The naturalist, Ivan Sanderson, had seemed to think the samples he examined were from a hitherto unclassified creature.

"However, it's only fair to say most scientists scoff at the possibility."

While Eads was speaking, Bud had held his breath. His face was almost purple when Grammy winked at him. "Maybe Mr. Eads would like to see what you found."

Bud exhaled explosively, leaped to his feet, and dashed in and back out of the camper. "Is what you found like this?"

Eads rose slowly, towering over Bud. "Identical!" He fingered the mass carefully. Then he smiled wryly at Grammy. "I tramped these mountains for six years without ever making a find like this, and this lad—" He was too overwhelmed to continue for a few seconds. "May I photograph this?"

"Sure," Bud answered, delighted to share his find. "Don't you want to know where I found it?"

Eads admitted he did, but wasn't going to ask. That was Bud's secret.

Bud looked long and hard straight into Mr. Eads' eyes. Then he said to Grammy, "Mr. Ward made me tell exactly where, and so did Jim Finch. It's all right to tell Mr. Eads, isn't it?"

Grammy thought he should tell Mr. Eads everything.

Bud hesitated. "D'you mind sitting down? I get a crick in my neck looking up at you." After the man was seated, Bud described what he and his grandmother had seen the previous afternoon, and what he had discovered earlier that morning, including the cigarette stub. Then he dashed into the camper and returned with his pictures. "I think I—we—found Bigfoot's lair." He grinned. "I guess that's the word. It sounds more 'lurky' than den."

"Either lair or den is suitable."

After studying the prints appreciatively, the photographer remarked, "You just might have found Bigfoot's lair." He rolled the cigarette butt between his fingers. "This tells me something I'd rather not put into words at the moment. Now, to ask a favor, would you show me the den?"

Bud was more than willing. "We can go right now."

"You're forgetting our date with the Neilsons," Grammy reminded him.

A crafty look gleamed in Bud's eyes. "I could tell them that you and I and Mr. Eads are going to hike straight up the mountain, but they're welcome to come." He hurried off, and returned shortly with a satisfied smirk on his face. "They don't want to climb a mountain." He looked around. "Where's Mr. Eads?"

"Gone to fetch his camera. What say we get ready, too?"

When Mr. Eads return, he had on hiking boots, and his photographic equipment in a canvas backpack. So did Bud, although his was a knapsack which lacked a frame. He had a sackful of pancakes hanging from his belt. "Grammy says I should lead the way. You follow me."

Grammy patted her rifle. "And I'll protect the two of you."

Bud led the way to the creek and turned upmountain. When they reached the game trail, he explained why he wanted to turn left. "I got to check on the pancakes I left by the creek yesterday."

"Pancakes!" Eads chuckled. "I thought those were our lunch."

Less than a minute afterward Bud shouted, "Grammy, they're gone!" He pointed to where he had seen them earlier that morning. "D'you s'pose Bigfoot ate them?"

"Let's try to find out." Eads examined the ground carefully. Then he stepped on a rock upstream to cross to the far bank without getting his feet wet. Bud and Grammy followed until he motioned them to hold back. He disappeared into the forest, and when he returned, he was mopping his face. "Not a track in sight. There's no telling what ate your bait. Could have been a crow, or deer, or even a bear."

"But not Bigfoot?"

Eads didn't think so.

Bud's shoulders sagged for a moment. "I'm still going to leave some more bait." He recrossed the creek and placed two pancakes where the others had been. Once more he resumed the lead and did not pause until he could point to an overturned tree and exclaim, "Here we are. That's Bigfoot's lair!"

12

· · ·

Stepping in Bigfoot's Footstep

The photographer slipped off his backpack and assembled his camera, attaching a wide-angle lens and flash cartridge. He also placed a flashlight in his hip pocket. Bud, following suit with his equipment, was about to step forward when Eads said, "Let me photograph the ground first." Quickly he did so from three positions—knee height, eye level, and with arms raised and camera aimed at the ground; next, he photographed the overhanging roots. Not until he used the flashlight to see that the hole was empty did he allow Bud and Grammy to join him. All three knelt down and leaned over the edge.

Bud pointed. "See the moss . . . and that thready stuff . . ."

"Inner bark fiber," Eads told him.

". . . and that small bough. A bear wouldn't drag that down in there, would it?"

The photographer played the light along the bough. "Hard to tell." He scanned the walls slowly.

"Hey, wait!" Bud exclaimed. "Shine the beam back on the bottom." He reached in his back pocket and pulled out his pictures. "Good thing I brought these. Something's different." He studied his film, then squinted hard below. "The bough in my picture is pointed in a different direction. It's been moved!" He wailed, "Oh, criminy, if Mr. Ward or Jim Finch crawled down in there, they've left their scent, and Bigfoot will stay away."

Grammy studied Bud's picture. "The boy is right."

Their friend stretched out on his stomach and leaned farther over the edge so the beam of his flashlight was concentrated on the bottom. After a moment he asked Bud to hand him his camera. He took two exposures, wriggled back, and got to his feet. "Don't move, either of you. I've got a hunch, and it's a nasty one." He rummaged about for a dead branch, peeled it, and knelt again between Grammy and Bud. "Keep the light focused on that bough," he asked, handing Bud the flashlight. Then he stretched out on his stomach and with both hands grasping the branch, brought the other end down hard on the bough.

Immediately there was a frightful-sounding metallic snap, and the end of the limb was crushed between the steel jaws of a large trap. "Thought so!" Eads murmured grimly.

Grammy moaned, "Oh, Buddy! If you'd crawled down in there this morning, you . . . you . . ." She couldn't finish.

Bud gulped. "Shucks, I'm no dummy. I know enough not to crawl in a strange hole! There could have been a rattlesnake in there."

"There was a rattlesnake down there, a two-legged one," Eads remarked angrily.

"Ye-ah," Bud agreed, "and I want proof! Hang on to me." While Mr. Eads gripped his belt, he took a picture. Then Eads took two more. All three sat up and asked each other, "Now, what'll we do?"

After a moment Eads asked if Bud had brought along the cigarette stub. He had. Eads told him to place it as close as possible to where he had found it. When Bud did so and backed out of range of the lens, Eads photographed it. "Put it back in your pocket, and don't lose it."

Bud did so, his eyes sparkling. "Are we gathering evidence?"

"We just might be." He asked Bud to go through the same motions he had made on earlier visits.

130

Bud climbed the tree trunk and peered down through the exposed roots, with the older man recording every move on film. "The pancakes I put up here haven't been touched. Should I leave more?"

"No, come down and let me get up there." Eads filmed from that position and jumped to the ground. "Say, I haven't taken any pictures of you and your grandmother by the tree. How about a nice pose?"

Bud pulled in his stomach, thrust out his chest and grinned broadly, saying "Che-e-e-ese!"

"Relax," Eads advised, smiling. He photographed the two, and then used the Polaroid to take another for them. Next he had Bud show him the tree trunk from which the moss had been stripped. Bud leaped to the spot. "Hold it right there!" Eads pointed to a heavily-trampled shrub. "Did you break that off?"

Bud was certain he had not.

"Step on this one next to it, and bounce lightly."

Bud did so. The unbroken shrub bore his weight.

Next Eads tested his weight on it, and the shrub resisted healthily. "Hmmm . . . something very heavy broke down the other one. Let's look about for big tracks."

Bud's eyebrows disappeared under his touseled hair. "You think Bigfoot crushed that bush?"

"Bigfoot, or a bear."

However, a diligent search revealed no unusual tracks.

Eads then decided to return to camp for a different camera equipped with a battery-driven intervalometer. He and the boys would return, set it up in a hidden place, and activate the timer to photograph the mouth of the burrow at brief intervals for the next twenty-four hours. "No matter who or what comes to this tree, daytime or nighttime, we'll have a record of it. So, it's important that you keep away."

Bud promised. "What should we do until tomorrow?"

The photographer hoped they would explore westward beyond the creek. "You'll come out about where the loggers are working. Someone will give you a ride back to camp."

Since that was agreeable, all returned to camp. Bud added a plastic bottle of water and a packet of raisins to his backpack, and stuffed some colored yarn in his pocket. "You're not nervous about hunting some more, are you?"

Grammy didn't know why she should be nervous.

"Well, if what Mr. Eads says is true about seeing Bigfoot's tracks in the logging area—"

Grammy would like to see a real monster track, and the closer it was, the better. "Save us a lot of hiking. At my age, that's good news."

Bud remembered to write their names and the direction they were taking on the list tacked to the bulletin board. Neither Mr. Ward, nor Jim Finch, nor any other members of the expedition were to be seen. Soon Bud and Grammy crossed the creek and made their way along the game trail. It meandered around big trees, doubled back at times, dribbled out in places, and became increasingly difficult to follow. Bud left numerous pieces of yarn along the way. Suddenly the trail veered off up the mountainside. After a long stiff climb Grammy was a little short of breath. "Let's rest and have a drink," she urged, wiping perspiration from her forehead.

The two sat down and leaned against a tree. Bud finally murmured, "I like to sit and listen. The longer you do it, the more you see and hear."

"And the harder it is to get up." Grammy stood up. "We'll never find Bigfoot just sitting and admiring the scenery."

Their progress was slow. An hour passed before they came unexpectedly onto an opening in the forest. This was not a clearing, but a thousand-foot-wide rock slide. They stepped out onto it gingerly, shading their eyes against the brilliant sunlight, and gazed up the mountain. Far above them they could see a gap in a high steep outcropping of rock. Apparently a portion of the cliff had sheered off, followed by tons of rock thundering down the slope, totally devastating a broad swath from the summit to another shelf of rock below.

"Grammy, I got an idea. See those cliffs on the far

side? I bet there's caves or shelters along the base of them. Let's check them out."

Grammy said it would be next to impossible to climb up the rock slide. The ground was too unstable. It would be better to cross over into the forest and ascend through the trees.

The sun was so hot that Bud couldn't wait to reach the shade. He started across the slide area, but found the going immediately difficult. Rocks slid out from under his feet, and rolled down the mountainside. When he pressed his weight against a small boulder while inching around it, it gave way suddenly and started a small avalanche of rocks and debris. Farther along a huge uprooted cedar lay prone across his path. Bud hauled himself along the remnants of a limb to the trunk, straddled the top, and then turned to help Grammy climb. "Want to rest?" he asked considerately.

"No, keep going. I'm nervous as a flea. If there's anything I don't want, it's a toboggan ride on a tree trunk down this mountain."

Bud eased to the ground and was about to step forward when he shrieked, "Look!"

Thinking he was in danger, Grammy grabbed his shirt. "Hold on! Dig in your heels."

Bud put his foot down carefully. "Look, look!" He was so excited he could only screech and point.

Grammy looked, and gasped. "Glory be! A monster track!"

In the soft dirt churned up by the avalance was a deeply impressed imprint of a giant-sized, five-toed foot with humanlike elongated heel and arch. "Oh, golly, I almost stepped in Bigfoot's footstep! Quick. Get my camera out of my pack." When Grammy handed it to him, Bud's hands shook so, he couldn't focus properly. The monster track was pointed toward them, indicating that the large creature had crossed the slide from the far side and apparently stepped over the tree and continued eastward. "I didn't bring a tape measure."

"Use the yarn." At that moment several small rocks bounded past them. "Hurry."

Bud finally managed to take a picture. Grammy took another of Bud while he carefully measured a piece of yarn the length of the footprint. Then he cut the yarn with his knife, and then another to show the width across the ball of the foot. "I can't believe it," he kept saying. "I found a real monster track!" He rolled the yarn around a finger and then placed it in his shirt pocket. He was so overjoyed that he forgot, and jumped up and down. Immediately the ground under his feet shifted so that Bud had to leap away from it.

"Keep going!" Grammy shouted, following at his heels.

Both were relieved to reach the far side. But there hiking proved increasingly difficult. At times their progress was measured in feet, rather than yards. Although Bud had a compass in his backpack, he didn't need to use it to keep from getting lost. Instead, he and his grandmother watched the direction of the sun's rays filtering down through gaps opened by fallen trees. When Bud suggested they climb to the base of the overhanging cliff, Grammy checked her watch. "It's too late in the day. I'd rather you talked with Mr. Eads first before going up there. Maybe he's already explored the area."

"I'm not afraid of going up there alone."

Grammy smiled. "Of course, you're not afraid, and neither am I. But seeing that footprint kind of made me believe Bigfoot might be real, after all."

Bud was shocked. How could Grammy ever doubt the creature existed? Still, seeing the track made him willing to talk to Tom Eads before struggling needlessly on his own to the mountaintop. The two continued on through the forest until they heard men's voices and at intervals the high whine of a power-driven saw. However, it took them another half hour before they stepped out into the opening created by the logging. The fallers and buckers, the men trimming the sawed-off trees, weren't as surprised at their appearance as Bud thought they might be. He quickly found out why.

The sawyer making an undercut in a huge yellow pine called out, "Howdy! How'd it go? Did you see Bigfoot?"

"Not today," Bud answered, grinning. "But we saw his track."

The man nodded. "Woods're full of 'em. Had a few around here this morning." He pointed his thumb toward the loading crane. "Guess they're all rubbed out by now."

Bud wailed. "Didn't you tell anybody?"

"Got no time." The man leaned toward the cut and turned on the gasoline-powered chain saw.

"I could have gotten another picture," Bud complained, after they had walked a hundred yards and could hear each other over the noisy saw. "How do you like that? Monster tracks all around, and that man couldn't care less."

Grammy thought that was because the loggers worked on a contract; that is, they were paid for the footage of lumber cut and hauled out. Probably the crew had been hampered in the past by monster hunters, and wasn't going to encourage others to wander about where falling trees presented a real danger. "Of course, the man could be pulling your leg. There might not be any tracks around here."

Bud remembered what he had been told about the Indians liking to pull jokes on white persons. The sawyer, and the rest of the crew, were all Indians.

At the loading landing, he and Grammy watched a log being lifted off the ground and, guided by cables, slowly lowered onto the bed of a logging truck. When it was safe to approach, Grammy asked the driver for a ride down the mountain.

Before answering, the driver tightened wrappers, or cables, over the logs stacked on his truck and also attached binders to keep the load from slipping. Then he thumbed back his hard hat. "Sure. Climb in the cab." He winked at Bud. "Catch any monsters today?"

Bud told about seeing the footprint. "I took a picture of it. Want to see it?"

"Naw." The man busied himself slipping a soiled red flag on the end of his load. Grammy and Bud climbed into the truck cab and relaxed on the cushioned seat. When the driver joined them, he asked, "Where you folks staying?"

Bud told him. "Do you live around here?"

The driver started the motor and let it idle for a few moments. He watched in the side mirror as the huge metal clamp and all cables were pulled free from his load. "I run the campground at the mouth of Bluff Creek," he said over his shoulder.

Grammy said she and Bud had camped there. "You must be Ella's father."

The driver turned. "Yeah. How do you know Ella?"

"Her dog tore up my new shirt," Bud said bluntly.

The man grunted. "She told me." Then he said to Grammy, "She said you were a nice lady."

"Ella is a very special girl," Grammy assured him, though she wasn't certain the man heard. He had turned back to look in the side mirror. Suddenly he leaned out, hollered, and slipped the stick down under into low-low gear. The huge engine throbbed, the truck labored into motion, jiggled over the rough ground, and eased out onto the roadway.

Meanwhile Bud remembered something Ella had told him. He shouted over the growling motor, "Ella said her brother and grandfather camp up here in the summer."

"My grandfather. Her great-grandfather."

"Where is his camp?"

Ella's father jerked his left thumb. "Way up there."

"Could we go see him?"

"You'd never find it," the man answered while slipping the stick forward into a higher gear.

Grammy leaned forward and shouted, "Could you give us a clue? We'd like to meet them. What could we take them?"

"Nothing. My boy Sam comes down to the landing once a week for grub." The driver said nothing more until he brought the heavy load to a halt three miles down the road. Grammy and Bud got out, thanking him for the lift, and asking him to say hello to Ella. He waved off. "Luck!"

As Grammy and Bud walked the ruts into the

campground they saw Mr. and Mrs. Neilson sitting in canvas chairs outside their camper.

"See anything interesting?" Mr. Neilson called out.

Although Bud ached to tell about discovering the monster track and show his picture, he called back, "Just a lot of trees." When he stepped over to the bulletin board to cross off his and Grammy's names, Mr. Ward called from inside his tent, "See anything interesting?"

Since the leader couldn't see his face, Bud stuck out his tongue. "Nothing but trees," he answered, feeling very smug. He caught up with his grandmother as she was unlocking the camper door. "I checked the list for tonight. We go in Mr. Neilson's truck again, and Mr. Ward's name isn't on either list. Now what do we do?"

The first item on the agenda, Grammy informed him, was to measure the bits of yarn and find out how big Bigfoot's footprint was.

One strand was twenty-two inches long, the other seven and three-eighths inches wide. Grammy pulled a paper bag out from under the sink, drew the dimensions of the huge foot, and cut it out. She placed it on the floor. "Put your foot on that, and I'll trace your measurements." Bud's foot was nine and one-half inches long and three and one-half inches wide at the ball of the foot.

140

"Wow, wow, wow!" he exclaimed, laughing at the comparison. "Wait'll I show Doug and Ronnie this. They'll turn green with ivy."

"Envy."

"Envy what?"

"They'll turn green with envy, not ivy."

"Who cares?" Bud gloated over the drawing. "I wish we'd had time to look for the other footprints. Too bad there was only one."

Grammy told him not to think about going back across the rock slide to look for more. Chances were the track they were fortunate enough to see had been wiped out by now.

Bud peered out the window. "Mr. Eads' camp looks deserted. Criminy, I want to talk to him. I wonder where he is?"

"Probably hunting for Bigfoot."

"What'll we do now?"

The next item on the agenda, Grammy said, was to change into their swim suits and bathe in the creek. She wrinkled her nose. "We stink as bad as Bigfoot, I bet."

Afterwards, while the meatloaf and potatoes were baking and Grammy was reading, Bud sat outside. He watched Mr. Ward's campsite intently. By no stretch of the imagination could he see any suspicious behavior there. Jim Finch was nowhere in sight. He hoped Mr. Finch hadn't gone to check the trap, found it sprung, and set it again. Then he remembered that Mr. Eads' camera would record the action, and smiled. Serve both of them right to be caught in a cruel act.

Next Bud thought what he would do if Mr. Ward slipped away, and he had to trail the teacher. By the time he dashed into the camper to put on his hiking boots, Mr. Ward could disappear in half a dozen different directions "I better get ready right now." Bud entered the camper quietly because Grammy was snoring. He put on his boots, snapped the flashlight to his belt, and checked his camera. Then he returned to his spying post. Like it or not, there was nothing to do but sit and wait for something to happen.

13
• • •

"There's Bigfoot!"

Finally it was six-thirty, time to report for the evening monster hunt. As people milled about the pickups, Bud kept an eye on Mr. Ward. Then he relaxed when he saw the leader place a rifle and large flashlight in the back of Mr. Neilson's truck. On arriving at the logging landing everybody searched for monster tracks. Bud kept muttering, "There's got to be some. The loggers said the woods were full of them." He had to grit his teeth to keep from bragging, "I know. I saw a dandy one."

Much to his and everyone else's disappointment, none were discovered. Bud whispered glumly to his grandmother, "I think that man with the saw told us a big fat fib, saying the woods were full of tracks."

143

"The woods *are* full of tracks," Grammy pointed out. "The joke is on us for thinking he meant only monster tracks."

Two hours had passed when Mr. Ward summoned the group to gather about him. He talked about the Hoopa Indians, and other tribes, who were established along the Klamath River long before white men prospecting for gold swarmed into the canyon, in the early 1850s. Before that time, the Hoopas claimed, their people frequently saw the hairy man-like giants. They called them *Oh-Mah,* or *Omah,* which meant something like "man-wild creature," using the same word for males and females of all ages. They thought of them as brothers and sisters with whom they shared the forest, fish, and water, but wild ones to be left alone. When the gold-seekers drove the Indians from the river, *Omah* fled, too. After the miners stripped the gold and departed, the Indians returned to their despoiled camps and took up their old ways again. But not *Omah.* Ever after, *Omah* kept his distance.

While Bud was fascinated with the story, he felt a twinge of jealousy. He thought Ella had revealed a very special secret when she told him and Grammy about *Omah.* He thought they knew something the others didn't. Yet here was Mr. Ward telling stories about numerous individual sightings of the hairy giant. Bud was also unhappy to hear Mr. Ward cau-

144

tion his listeners: white persons had no way of knowing for certain whether the Hoopa stories were about a real flesh-and-blood creature, or a spirit being who figured in their myths, or whether the Indians deliberately made up the stories to fool white folks.

"Any questions?" the leader asked when he finished speaking.

"I've got one," Bud blurted. "What are you going to do if you see Bigfoot?"

Mr. Ward admitted he would try to capture him one way or another.

"You mean, shoot him?"

Personally, Mr. Ward stated, he hoped killing wouldn't be necessary. However, as much as he disliked the idea, he felt one of the creatures must be sacrificed so scientists could study it.

Bud was shocked at the teacher's attitude. So were some, but not all, of the others. Grammy wondered aloud if Mr. Ward had considered the injury to a small family group if one of its members was captured or killed.

Yes, he had, the teacher admitted. But one must consider that all wild creatures suffered injuries and death. Once there was undeniable proof that the wild giants were real, then measures would be taken to protect them. Right now they were in real peril, he said, because so many people were hunting them throughout western British Columbia, Washington,

Oregon, and northern California. In all those millions of square miles, only one small area, Skamania County in Washington, prohibited the killing of a Bigfoot or Sasquatch.

"I'd shoot him on sight," Mr. Neilson stated unashamedly. "A man could make a fortune selling the carcass or displaying it at carnivals."

A young man, one of the motorcyclists, asked thoughtfully, "Does science have to be served by caging a wild creature, or depriving it of life? If Bigfoot exists, he's a rare and precious being. Why can't we press to have legislation passed to protect the species without capturing or killing one first? I mean, y'know, if we can save the grizzly or trumpeter swan from extinction, why callously threaten Bigfoot?"

"But we don't have to prove that the grizzly or trumpeter swan exists," Mr. Ward argued. "We can't protect Bigfoot now because too many important people feel the Bigfoot-Sasquatch story is a hoax."

Bud scowled, though no one could see his face in the dark. "Maybe it's better to kill Bigfoot than to set a trap and have him bleed to death when his foot gets chewed up in a bear trap!"

No one except Grammy realized Bud's remark was aimed at Mr. Ward. Apparently the teacher didn't either, or purposely ignored it. He suggested everyone return to the truck. Two more hours passed mostly in sitting and waiting, driving up and down the road, and more sitting and waiting. However, at one stop midway between the campsite and logging landing, everyone heard noises far off in the woods.

Thump . . . thump . . . crackle . . . thump . . .

"Something's prowling about out there!"

"Maybe it's Bigfoot!"

"Aw, cool it. That's a bear."

Bud broke out in goosepimples from his ears to his ankles. "Criminy, I didn't bring my tape recorder."

"Quiet! Listen!" Mr. Ward urged as he groped for his flashlight.

Thump . . . thump . . . crackle . . . thump . . . The sounds appeared to be those of a heavy-footed creature coming closer and closer. The moment Mr. Ward beamed the light in that direction, all heard a loud snort. Then the sounds faded off in the distance.

Everybody talked at once:

"That was Bigfoot!"

"Naw, that was a bear."

"Mr. Ward, you shouldn't have turned on the flashlight."

"He should, too. D'you want that monster climbing on the truck?"

"Let's get out of here!"

Even though it seemed darker than ever after Mr. Ward turned off his flashlight, Grammy could tell Bud was shaking. She told him to calm down, and stop biting his fingernails.

By eleven o'clock everyone was weary from the strain of suspenseful listening. Obviously whatever creature had made those noises had gone away. No one objected when Mr. Ward decided it was time to return to camp. Mr. Neilson started the engine, switched the headlights on high, and drove slowly down the rutted logging road. Bud was so sleepy he leaned his head on Grammy's shoulder and closed his eyes. Thus he did not see a huge glistening dark figure loom up in the glare of the headlights.

"There's Bigfoot!" someone shouted.

Bud jerked upright. "Where? Where?"

"There!"

Mrs. Neilson screamed as an enormous hairy creature lunged across the road in two long strides. It glared fiercely into the lights and plunged out of sight into the forest.

Mr. Neilson jerked on the emergency brake and removed a rifle from the gun rack at the back of the cab. He stepped out quickly for so fat a person, and pumped several shots in the creature's direction. Mr. Ward was equally swift raising his rifle, but did not fire it. The others shouted, and blinked flashlights, but none left the truck to pursue the beast.

148

Talk exploded like popcorn kernels in hot oil:

"That wasn't a bear. Bears have snouts."

"It had a face like a gorilla."

"Did you see how his coat glistened in the light?"

"What a stride! I couldn't believe my eyes. He crossed the road in two leaps!"

"Did you see his hands? They were huge!"

"The upper part of his arms were as big as hams!"

Bud jumped up and down, hugging Grammy and screeching, "We saw him, we saw him, we saw Bigfoot! Boy, I sure wish Ronnie was here. He could see for himself that was no man in a monkey suit."

Only Mr. Neilson voiced bitter disappointment. "Why didn't you shoot?" he complained angrily to Mr. Ward. "You had a better chance at him than I did."

Mr. Ward seemed to be in a state of partial shock. "I don't know why I didn't shoot, but I just couldn't."

The others robustly complimented the leader on not shooting. All except Mr. Neilson. "You just let a million bucks get away from you!"

"I couldn't shoot that creature." Mr. Ward tried to make him understand. "I just could . . . not . . . press the trigger."

Everyone dropped to the road and knelt alongside the awesome tracks. But no one had brought a camera, nor material to make a plaster cast, nor even a tape measure. At last Mr. Ward suggested the group return in the morning, very early, before the logging traffic resumed. That seemed sensible, since no one knew how far away in the dark Bigfoot had fled, or whether he might have slipped back to spy on them.

As Grammy and Bud walked toward their camper, Bud wondered aloud, "I bet Mr. Eads will be disappointed when he finds out he missed seeing Bigfoot. I wonder where he was all day."

"He's back. I saw his truck when Mr. Neilson turned into the campground. We'll find out tomorrow."

"Should I go over and tell him now?"

Since the photographer's campsite was dark, Grammy would not let Bud disturb him. "You better hustle to bed if you're going to be up at daybreak." As they entered the camper, she asked Bud if he still planned on sleeping outside.

"Sure. Why not?"

Bigfoot had been seen little more than a mile away.

"Aw, he's long gone now. Boy, I'd like to fix that Mr. Neilson, shooting off that rifle!" Still, after slipping into his pajamas, Bud picked up a can of snuff, his camera, and flashlight. "See you in the morning."

"Sleep tight."

Bud did. At first light Monday morning he was so deep in sleep that he did not hear Mr. Eads leave a note under the blade of the windshield wiper. However, the sound of his truck leaving did waken Bud. He scrambled out of his covers and waved his arms, but the photographer did not stop. Finding the note did not make Bud feel any better. The message read: *Changed the film. Nothing to report yet. See you tonight.*

Grammy called out, "What's going on?"

Bud entered the camper, complaining because Mr. Eads had driven off.

"Which direction?"

"Up the road." He whistled. "Someone must have told him we saw Bigfoot last night. How else would he know?"

After a moment Grammy said, "Maybe he doesn't know. Or maybe he heard the rifle shots and figured someone was shooting at Bigfoot."

Bud pouted. "I wanted to check the lair this morning."

Grammy thought he wanted to try and locate Ella's brother and great-grandfather. When Bud's face cleared, she said, "Then let's go. Or do you want to take time to make pancakes?"

Bud wavered. "I should check the ones I left by the creek." When he peered out the window and saw several cookfires going, he decided, "I'd rather beat the others up the road."

After a hasty breakfast Grammy started to pack a

151

lunch. Bud objected to her making bologna and peanut butter sandwiches. "Ella said her great-grandfather was living the old way. Maybe we better take Indian-type food." While she filled small plastic bags with dried fruit, dried beef jerky, raisins, nuts, and granola, he added candy bars and snuff, in case they encountered Bigfoot.

Grammy placed the articles in the small canvas knapsack which had shoulder straps but no frame. "Food . . . candy, snuff . . . matches. Hand me the flashlight. Knife?"

Bud patted the sheath hooked into his belt. "Got it." He snapped his fingers. "Almost forgot the tape measure and yarn." He stuffed both in a pocket.

"Whenever Grampy and I planned to visit an Indian or Eskimo camp, we always took a gift. The old man might like the snuff. How about a couple of your comic books for Sam?"

"Sam?"

"Ella's brother. And what about the tape recorder?"

"Put it in. I'll carry the pack. You'll have enough, carrying the rifle." He added a plastic container of water, and closed the pack.

The two left quietly and soon reached the spot where Bigfoot had crossed the road. Bud was surprised Mr. Eads wasn't there, taking photographs. "Thank goodness, he didn't run over Bigfoot's tracks." Bud shrugged off the light pack and set to work measuring and photographing one of the footprints. The dimensions were the same as the one he had seen on the rock slide. Since he had used up a container of film, he slipped in a new one. Then he and Grammy hiked on. Not long after they heard a truck approaching. It was the pickup transporting the logging crew to work. "Climb in back," the driver invited them. When they did, one of the crew asked, "Going monster hunting again?"

Bud pretended to be indifferent. "No, we saw him last night." Secretly he was very disappointed when none of the men asked for details. It was Grammy who said they planned to hike to the Indian camp. Could anyone show them where to start?

"Ella's father bet we couldn't find it," Bud said.

All eyes turned on him. "You know Ella?"

"Do I know Ella? Her dog chewed up my new shirt!"

The men laughed. "We heard about that," one said. "Ella rides up to the landing once a week with grub for her brother. He hikes down the mountain for it. Gives him a break. Ella told us about the nice old . . ." The man corrected himself hastily, "the nice white-haired lady."

Another remarked, "If Ella said you're a nice lady, we believe it!"

Grammy smiled. She knew how Indians loved to

talk, and pass the word along about things they saw or heard. "We have some comic books for Sammy, and snuff for the old man."

The men exchanged glances. When the truck stopped alongside the loading crane, one of the loggers helped Grammy to the ground. "I'll start you out," he volunteered. He walked Grammy and Bud to a path, hidden from the clearing by a tall shrub but easily seen taking off up through the timber. "It's a long hike, so take it easy. Sammy's got it blazed to the top of the mountain. Come back down by four, and we'll give you a ride back to your camp. You'll need it."

"That's very nice of you. We'll do that," Grammy promised as she and Bud headed into the forest.

14

• • •

A Plan to Save Bigfoot

Bud stopped frequently to blaze the trail with bits of yarn. While he could read the signs scattered along the way by either Ella's brother or great-grandfather, he enjoyed making his own. Besides, the bright red yarn was easier to see than a clump of moss here, a peeled stick there, or slashed bark. As on previous days, Bud learned that the woods were not full of Bigfoot tracks. At least, he didn't see any. When he and Grammy stopped to rest, she asked, "Now that you've simmered down from last night's excitement, how do you feel about this Bigfoot business? You think he's real? You're certain what you saw last night was not a bear."

"That was no bear," Bud stated flatly.

"Will Ronnie and Doug believe you saw Bigfoot? What will you do if they make fun of you, or call you a liar?"

"I'll punch 'em both in the nose," Bud said, grinning.

"But they might not be the only ones who won't believe you saw a monster," she cautioned. "You can't fight the whole world. You better think about it."

Bud not only thought about it; he talked to himself. He had been so busy looking for Bigfoot that he really hadn't had a good talk with himself for days. It seemed like months since he came to Bluff Creek, not just days. "Use the ol' bean, Miller. Grammy's right. You can't fight the whole world." There were two good reasons why he couldn't do that: first, he didn't like to fight; he didn't like having people mad at him, or making fun of him. Second, he knew he wasn't the world's greatest fighter for his age and weight. But nobody was going to tell him he hadn't seen the monster. "Stick to your guns, Miller." Several times in the next hour of climbing, he stopped and carried on a serious conversation with himself. Grammy wisely refrained from noticing, until he told her, "I got it all worked out in my mind."

She suggested Bud tell her about it.

Bud figured most people who believed in Bigfoot's existence, or that Sasquatch monster up north, were the ones who had seen a Bigfoot or Sasquatch. "They know he's real. Like us. No one can tell us we didn't see a monster. But some folks don't need to see Bigfoot himself. They became believers after they saw his footprints, or even Roger Patterson's photograph. Us believers don't care what scientists say about it being impossible for a Bigfoot to exist. We know different. So I think what we need is more believers. But not ones like Mr. Neilson. We don't want the kind who shoot for money, or would put Bigfoot in a cage. I don't want that to happen . . . ever! I want to help save Bigfoot from people like that."

Helping protect Bigfoot was an enormous, complicated task, Grammy pointed out gently. What could he do?

Bud was not the least discouraged. He knew exactly where to start. "First, you got to make people believe. Okay. If Mr. Eads could take lots and lots of pictures of Bigfoot and his family . . . y'know, walking and fishing and eating, stuff like that . . . then more folks will have to believe he's real. Second, when more folks see how special he is, they'll want to protect him. They'll work hard, I bet, to have laws passed to save him from hunters like Mr. Neilson."

"But what will you do? Take pictures, too?"

Bud hugged himself, his eyes sparkling with excitement. "Sure! See, I don't think that lair under the cedar tree is Bigfoot's regular one. So, I'm going to ask Ella's great-grandfather to show Mr. Eads and me where Bigfoot and his family really hide out. Then we'll sneak up close, and fix a blind to hide in, and take pictures! Isn't that a neat idea?" he burbled.

"Well, it's certainly worth a try," Grammy assured him. "Keep your fingers crossed and hope Ella's great-grandfather will help you. And don't be mad if he won't. He may not know anything more about Bigfoot than you do."

The two continued their hike. Not long after, they heard strange noises from afar. Both stopped, and listened carefully. Finally Bud whispered, "That sounds like singing."

The tuneless three-note chanting, punctuated by high-pitched yelps, lured them on to the edge of a mountain meadow. The singer was there, a thin elderly Indian sitting cross-legged on the ground. As he chanted, he shook a feathered rattle.

"Why is he chanting?"

Grammy thought he might be communicating with brother spirits. These could be birds, trees, animals, rocks, the wind, sun . . . anything in nature or the spirit world of the Hoopas.

"Could he be communicating with Bigfoot?" Bud listened attentively, and then hummed softly in an effort to memorize the chant. "Ronnie would get a kick out of this. Too bad he isn't here." Suddenly Bud remembered the tape recorder. Why not tape the chanting? An even more delicious idea squirreled through his brain. "Watch this." He removed the battery-operated tape recorder from the knapsack, plugged in the small hand-held microphone, and pressed the Record and Forward buttons. As the tape in the cassette moved, he imagined he was facing a television camera, saying, "Hel-lo, everybody. This is Bud Miller, high in the Siskiyou Mountains in northern California. This is Bigfoot country . . . uh . . . y'know, home of a fabulous hairy ape-type monster that keeps popping up alongside logging roads and scaring the heck out of people. I know! I saw him last night. I'm still shaking. Well, anyhow, here's a real Indian medicine man, chanting. He's trying to communicate with Bigfoot. Let's listen and see if he's . . . uh . . . if Bigfoot answers." Bud pointed the microphone toward the singer and moved the Volume button forward. After a minute's taping, he turned the microphone back to record his voice, "There it is, folks, a gen-u-ine medicine man chanting in the forest. Sorry Bigfoot didn't answer. Better luck next time." After Bud pressed the Stop button, he giggled. "That'll knock Ronnie off the planet."

"Oh, my," Grammy enthused, "you sounded just like a regular TV announcer."

Bud's eyebrows shot up. "Really? How about that? Maybe I better walk out there and interview the old man."

Grammy thought the old Indian would not like having his singing interrupted. It would be better to find his camp, and talk to Sam first.

The two moved around the meadow until Bud spied moisture-darkened ground. In following the narrow ribbon of seepage upmountain, he stopped so abruptly that Grammy bumped into him from behind. Bud pointed excitedly. An Indian youth wearing cutoff jeans, tennis shoes, a shoulder harness to which was fastened a transistor radio, and headphones was tossing a basketball into a wooden hoop nailed to a tree. He was a head taller than Bud, and well muscled. To one side was a shelter fashioned of cedar boughs laid across upright poles set in the ground. Underneath was a blanket roll, a sleeping bag, and a duffel bag. The fire pit contained a metal grate on which rested a long-handled frying pan and blackened stew pot. Tins and sacks of food, including a carton of crackers, were strewn on the ground. "This is living the old way?" Bud exclaimed, unable to mask his disappointment. "I could show that kid a thing or two about camping."

Grammy snorted. "He didn't learn camping from a manual. Now, mind your manners and announce yourself."

160

"Announce myself!"

Grammy explained that a stranger didn't walk into an Indian camp unannounced.

"Oh." Bud cupped his hands around his mouth and shouted. The youth, Sam, continued shooting baskets. Next Bud whistled sharply. Sam spied them and peeled the headphones from his ears. But he didn't speak.

"Are you Ella's brother?"

Sam nodded.

An awkward silence followed. Grammy poked Bud. "Tell him who you are."

Bud felt his cheeks getting hot. He didn't like having someone staring holes through him. "I'm Bud Miller. This is my grandmother. Ella told us to come see you."

Grammy added, "We brought a picnic lunch. Will you join us?"

Sam smiled, kicked some twigs aside, and sat on the ground. As Grammy set out the food, Bud handed Sam the comic books and a candy bar. Sam was pleased. "You just hiking around?" When the two nodded, he said, "You're not writers, are you, or reporters? Good! I'm so sick of reporters hiking up here to talk to Joe about Bigfoot. He fills 'em full of hokum. Course he puts on a good show—"

"Bigfoot does?" Bud interrupted excitedly.

"Naw. Joe."

"Who's Joe?"

"The old man." Sam pointed his thumb toward the meadow. "That's him, chanting."

"His name is Joe?" Bud wailed. He had taken it for granted the elderly Indian's name would be something impressive like Chief Kills His Bear. "Does he speak English?"

Sam looked at Bud as if he was stupid. "Why shouldn't he? He went to a mission school. He prefers Hoopa, but he can speak English if he wants to."

Grammy asked Sam if he spoke the Hoopa tongue.

Sam curled his lip. "Naw, none of us kids do. And don't ask me about the old times, or old myths, or old anything! Let's talk about baseball. Who's going to win the pennant?"

Bud and Sam discussed sports until Joe made his appearance. The moment he saw them, he raised his right hand, palm out, and intoned in a deep voice, "How! Welcome, strangers!" His eyes glittered.

Sam laughed. "He learned that watching Indians on television." He told the old man, "They aren't reporters. You don't have to put on a show."

Joe chuckled, and sat down. He removed a headband made of deerskin padded with grass, and decorated with the dried scalps of red-headed sapsuckers.

"We brought you something," Bud said, placing the can of snuff before him. When Joe ignored it,

Grammy offered him raisins and nuts. As he ate, she asked if she might examine the headband closely. He nodded indifferently.

Bud admired the old man's braids. Although his white hair was thin, the braids were filled out with strips of colored cloth, small tarnished bells, shells and beads strung on dried grass, and tufts of coarse hair. "What kind of animal hair have you got tied in your braids? Is that big tuft bear hair? Does your wearing it mean you killed a bear?"

Joe waggled four fingers, and then helped himself to the beef jerky.

"Four bears! Wow! With a bow and arrow?"

Sam guffawed.

Bud ignored Sam, and pointed to some long silky black hairs dangling from the end of the braids. "What's that?"

"Skunk. Here badger. Here eagle feather."

Next Bud's eyes focused on coarse brownish strands tinged with red. The sight of them made him break out in goosepimples. He reached over and touched them. "Moss?"

Joe shook his head. "Bear."

"Hunh-uh!" Bud said emphatically. "Too long for bear. What is it?"

The old man shrugged. "Don't remember."

Bud looked him straight in the eyes. "I've got some of that. It's Bigfoot hair, isn't it?"

Sam guffawed again. "Oh, corn! You're one of those nuts chasing Bigfoot. I should've known." He picked up a comic book and cut himself off from further conversation.

Bud's glance never wavered from the old man. "Ella said you would tell me about Bigfoot."

Grammy corrected Bud gently. "Ella said to ask you about *Omah*. We believe in *Omah*."

"We saw Bigfoot last night. I mean, *Omah*." Bud described the encounter.

"Why you come here?"

Bud raised his camera. "Maybe you'll tell me where Bigfoot is so I can take his picture."

Joe's eyes narrowed. "Make lots of money." He flicked a glance at Grammy's rifle. "You shoot 'im. Get more money."

"No!" Bud and Grammy chorused. One talked and then the other, assuring they meant no harm to the wild creature. Bud explained why taking pictures could help Bigfoot. "All we want is pictures. So does a good friend of ours. He doesn't carry a gun. All he shoots is a camera."

Joe folded his arms and was silent a long time. Suddenly he said, "You pay me, I show you *Omah* tomorrow maybe." He picked up the remaining sticks of jerky, the can of snuff, and motioned Sam to help him to his feet. Then he walked off into the woods.

Sam called back over his shoulder, "Hey, if you come tomorrow, will you bring some bologna sandwiches?" Then he followed the old man out of sight.

Bud and Grammy gathered up their belongings and headed down the trail. When Bud thought they were far enough away so as not to be overhead, he whooped, "Tomorrow, you bring heap big bologna sandwiches." After a good laugh, he added, "Boy, we sure learned a lot of nothing."

"You really didn't expect that old man to tell complete strangers anything really important, did you?"

Bud confessed he had. "I'm sure not hiking up this mountain tomorrow just so he can make fools of us."

Grammy claimed she'd climb the mountain again, out of curiosity to see what the old man would do. "He hasn't accepted us yet. Indians are always reserved with whites until they feel they can trust us. He just might have a lot to tell us."

"A lot of nothing," Bud grumped. As long as they were high on the mountainside, he wanted to walk to the base of the cliffs they had seen the day before.

Grammy checked her watch. She was agreeable, providing they reached the logging area by four o'clock. The two discovered nothing unusual, and guided by the bits of yarn Bud had left, made their way back down the mountain. The loggers greeted them like old friends. "You see old Joe, hey?"

Bud nodded. "He invited us to come back tomorrow."

"Sam asked me to bring bologna sandwiches," Grammy added.

The men laughed and said something in Hoopa tongue. "Sam's a good kid." Since it was quitting time, they gathered up their tools and accompanied Grammy and Bud to the pickup truck. On the ride down the mountain road, Bud pointed out where they had seen Bigfoot the previous evening.

"You see him, hey?" One said something in Hoopa, and then all laughed uproariously.

"I'm not joking. It was scary!"

Again the men laughed, but said nothing. The truck stopped at the campground, the driver barely giving Bud and Grammy time to jump down before pulling away.

The first thing Bud and Grammy noticed was that several cars and trucks not belonging to expedition members were parked around the campsite. "Mr. Eads is back!" Bud spurted ahead, calling the photographer's name, since no one was in sight. "Mr. Eads! It's Bud. Where are you?"

"In the tent. Be out in a minute." The moment he emerged, Bud shouted, "We saw Bigfoot last night. I got a picture of his footprint!"

Mr. Eads clapped Bud on the shoulder. "I heard about that. Afternoon, Mrs. Miller. I've got exciting news for you, too. Let's go inside the camper to talk. There's a man I want you to meet." He helped Bud slip off his knapsack and called through the screen door, "Harry, are you awake? Here's the young man I told you about." Moments later Eads introduced Grammy to a red-haired middle-aged man named Harry Elston. He had been napping in the bunk. "Harry is a long-time friend and newspaper reporter. We collaborate on writing magazine articles. He wants to interview you, Bud."

"Me?" Bud chirped. "Am I going to have my picture in the paper?"

"You bet. Sit down, sit down." Everyone bumped elbows jovially, and slipped onto the cushioned benches on each side of the small table. Mr. Eads brought cans of pop from the refrigerator and pulled off the tops.

As excited as Bud was, and anxious to talk, he gulped the cold drink first. Mr. Eads sat down across from him. "Things are a little hectic. To save work for Harry, let me talk first. Got your notepad, Harry? Good. Bud, I've got a surprise for you later on, so be patient. Now, you and your grandmother, Mrs. Miller—"

"Just call me Matty," Grammy interrupted.

"You two arrived here Saturday ahead of the oth-

167

ers in the Ward expedition. You found the lair, as you call it, that same afternoon."

"And the hank of hair."

"Right. You showed the hair to Mr. Ward, and that fellow named Jim Finch. After supper you hunted for Bigfoot between here and the logging landing. Neither of you saw nor heard anything unusual. Next morning, Sunday, you hiked alone back to the cedar tree, took pictures, found the cigarette stub. Came back, had breakfast. I came by, you told me your story, we went back to the fallen tree and took more pictures. Then we all came back here and went our separate ways. Got that, Harry?"

The newspaper reporter nodded without stopping his scribbling.

Next, Eads said, he and his son, Jack, returned to the cedar tree and set up the camera and intervalometer; returned to camp, got Phil and hiked down the mountain on the east side of the creek until they reached Bluff Creek. They walked up its banks very slowly, looking for footprints "and found sixteen! Sixteen, fresh, deep footprints in damp sand! Twenty-two inches long, left foot, right foot . . . I shot an entire roll of film. We didn't get back until almost seven, and by then you were off hunting again."

"And saw Bigfoot," Bud just had to say.

"Let me finish," Eads said nicely. "The boys and I made a fast trip down the mountain to the store at

Weitchpec. I called Harry at Eureka, told him what you and I had discovered, and urged him to come up here. Well, you know how it is with country telephones. Everybody listens in on the party line. Also, I had to talk pretty loud, so the people at the store overheard me. They must have told others something exciting was going on up at Bluff Creek. Anyway, we bought our grub, ate at a nearby fishing lodge, drove back fast, and were asleep before you returned."

"Didn't you hear Mr. Neilson shooting at Bigfoot?"

The answer was no. This morning, Mr. Eads continued, he hiked back to the tree, changed the film, and left the note for Bud. Then he, Jack, and Phil drove up the road, turned off on a logging road that went down to Bluff Creek, and spent the day prowling the creek bottom for a glimpse of Bigfoot. No luck. "By the time we returned here, Harry was waiting for us. He had talked to Mr. Ward and heard about your seeing Bigfoot last night. Mr. Neilson drove Harry up to see what was left of the footprints after all the truck traffic today. There was hardly anything to see. He came back here, we arrived, and now you're here. Your surprise must be about ready by now, Bud. You and Matty finish talking to Harry. Carry on." Eads bounded out of the camper and disappeared into the tent.

Bud was so excited he could hardly talk fast

enough. He told Harry Elston about the pancakes, and not being afraid to walk alone in the woods, and everything that had happened in the last two days. Grammy never once corrected him. By the time he finished, Mr. Eads was at the door with Jack and Phil. He had a bundle of newspapers in his hands which he placed very carefully on the table. He peeled back the papers, and then gloated: "How's that for a plaster cast of a monster track!"

Bud squealed, and bounced on the cushion. When he reached out to touch the plaster, Mr. Eads stayed his hand. "Let the plaster harden more."

Bud gloated over every inch. "Is this really for me? Can I take it home to show my pals?"

The answer was yes. "Now, see what Phil has for you."

Phil had developed the photographs taken at the cedar tree, including a fine one of Bud and Grammy standing proudly each side of the overhanging roots. "That print is for you. Phil made a complete set for the newspaper. Now, look at this. Careful! The prints are damp." Phil laid out a number of prints taken with the hidden camera. One filmed either just before dark or daylight showed the back of a huge dark broad-shouldered figure.

"Bigfoot!" Bud squealed again.

"Maybe. Only maybe," Mr. Eads stressed. "Much

as I'd like to say it was Bigfoot, I can't. It could be a bear."

"I'm so thankful you released that trap," Grammy said as she gazed at the picture of the cruel steel teeth. "I just hope whoever set it didn't return."

Mr. Eads said he hoped the same. The film had recorded other blurred objects which he assumed were deer, or possibly the huge creature passing in front of the lens. "If the trap-setter returned today, we'll have a picture of him tomorrow."

"Maybe we better go there now, and check," Bud worried aloud. "I mean, if the trap is set again, Bigfoot or a bear could get hurt tonight."

"That's too long a walk added to today's hike," Grammy told him.

Bud chewed his thumbnail, thinking furiously. He didn't want to forget anything Harry should know. "What about the second batch of pancakes I left by the creek?"

Jack thought a picture of Bud placing his pancakes there would have great human interest value. "How many people hunting Bigfoot use pancakes for bait?" he asked Harry.

"Let's go" Eads suggested, leaping up and out the door.

"What about the cast?" Bud asked.

"Leave it and the film to dry. We won't be gone long."

171

"Hold on, everybody." Grammy said she would rather start preparing supper. "You're all invited, but bring your own camp stools."

"We'll furnish the hamburger," Jack offered, taking a package out of the refrigerator. He and the others escorted Grammy to her camper, and then hurried off, with Bud in the lead.

About a half hour later, as she was putting a large apple pie in the oven, Mr. Ward knocked on the door. "You went off without signing the sheet this morning. I just came by to see that you're all right."

Grammy apologized. "The loggers knew where we were. If we hadn't come back by four, I think they would have told someone, or looked for us. But that's no excuse for not letting you know. We'll be going back up to the Indian camp in the morning."

"What Indian camp?"

Grammy explained about Joe and Sam. "The old man told Bud that if we came back tomorrow, he might tell us where Bigfoot was." She laughed. "I honestly don't think he knows any more than you or I do. By the way, I liked your talk about the Hoopas last night. Where did you hear all those stories about them?"

Mr. Ward smiled. "I didn't hear them. I read about them in old, old issues of the *Journal of American Folk-lore*. Well, see you tonight."

"Don't count on us. We're having company for dinner."

Mr. Ward waved off, and Grammy returned to her cooking.

15
• • •

"...high time Bigfoot learned to trust somebody"

"We were lucky! The pancakes weren't all eaten up, so Mr. Eads could take my picture standing by them," Bud reported the moment he returned from the creek. "Harry thought that was a neat idea, using pancakes for bait. He's going to say so in the article he's writing about me." He patted his chest. "Grammy, I'm going to be famous, after it's published, aren't I?"

Grammy laughed. "Even famous people have to wash their hands, and help serve supper."

The men arrived shortly, each with a canvas chair. Fortunately Harry brought his notepad and pen because Mr. Eads talked continuously about Bigfoot, and at the same time wolfed down hamburgers and pie. "I have a hunch something big is going to happen! Tonight, let's all ride in my truck. Jack, set the big camera on a tripod in the back, and use the heavy flash. Phil, you drive. Bud, bring your camera and tape recorder. Mrs. Miller—"

"Let me drive," Grammy urged. "Then the rest of you can be in the back and free to jump into action." She chuckled. "But I warn you. I have a fast foot when it comes to stomping on the brake."

Not long after, they all departed in Mr. Eads' truck. Grammy drove slowly up and down the road, and parked with the lights out whenever the photographer asked. But they neither heard nor saw Bigfoot.

"Better luck tomorrow. See you in the morning," Mr. Eads remarked after they returned to camp.

Bud yawned all the time he was undressing. He barely stayed awake long enough to zip up his sleeping bag.

Hours later he wakened, and instantly sensed something was wrong. Before he could think what might have disturbed his sleep, he heard far off to the east some frightening screaming. Scalp prickling, heart thumping, he sat up, straining to hear. The screams pierced the night again. Quickly Bud unzipped the bag, pulled on his boots and ran to the

175

camper door. "It's me," he called out before opening it, in case Grammy thought he was a prowler.

"Lock the door!" Grammy spoke urgently. "Don't turn on any lights. Fasten the windows." Meanwhile, shielding the flashlight with her hand, she lifted the rifle and ammunition from the closet, and switched off the light. Since the rear door faced the woods, she wedged the window so it opened a slot, providing just enough room for the rifle barrel.

The shrieking continued, and seemed a mite louder. It was a bone-chilling horrendous sound, one that could only be caused by terror or intolerable pain. Both Grammy and Bud sensed immediately what must have happened. The sounds came from the direction of the fallen cedar tree. Whoever had planted the big trap in the burrow must have set it again. Some creature had been caught in the cruel, sharp, steel jaws.

Bud began to cry. "That's Bigfoot screaming. He's hurt! We've got to help him. We've got to!"

"Stop it!" Grammy snapped before Bud became hysterical. "We don't know it's Bigfoot. It could be a bear or a mountain lion. Listen!" The sounds grew louder and more distinct. Whoever or whatever was making them must be nearing the campground.

Bud peered out the side window over the sink. "Oh, no! Mr. Ward has his lantern lighted. Hasn't he got better sense? The Neilson's lights are on, too. It's still dark at Mr. Eads."

176

"Not surprised," Grammy remarked. Mr. Eads would know better than to turn on lights.

Bud stepped to Grammy's side and peered through the open slot. Time after time he heard the anguished enraged sounds which varied from yelps to roars. He covered his ears, and stamped his feet in frustration. "Isn't there something we can do? We can't let Bigfoot suffer like that." Then Bud heard noises that brought him to the sink window again. "I can see Jim Finch. He's got his rifle and some rope. There's Mr. Neilson . . . and Mr. Ward. They've got guns, too. O-my-gosh, Grammy, come look! They're lighting a torch! Why do they need a torch?"

Grammy stretched to look. In the sputtering light of burning oil-soaked rags, she could see the armed party. "Wild animals are afraid of fire. The men must figure Bigfoot is out there, thrashing around, and this is their best chance to bring him down."

"Then they're the ones who set the trap!"

"I'm afraid so."

Bud wanted to open the door and yell at the three not to dare shoot Bigfoot. Grammy wouldn't let him. After all, like them or not, those men were risking injury to keep a wild creature from reaching the camp.

Bud hadn't thought of that. A human couldn't make those awful noises. Only a beast could.

"I'm beginning to think we're hearing a moun-

177

tain lion. Bears growl and roar. Cats shriek and scream."

The yowling continued for a while after the three men vanished. Then slowly the sounds diminished, and seemed to come from higher up on the mountain.

Bud guessed what had happened. "Bigfoot's dragging that trap up the mountain! He's not coming this way. But he's bound to leave a trail of blood, so Mr. Neilson won't have any trouble finding him."

"Could be," Grammy agreed. While relieved that their personal danger had lessened, she was very upset at the thought of a wounded creature, enduring excruciating pain, now forced to flee from hunters.

Bud had remained looking out the side window. "Someone in Mr. Eads' camper just flashed a light. I better answer." He blinked his flashlight several times. Almost immediately he saw a light moving in their direction. Grammy turned on the yellow outdoor light, and moments later Mr. Eads stepped inside.

"I wanted to make certain you were all right," he told them. He was fully dressed for hiking and had a knapsack on his back. "The boys and Harry and I are going to follow your friends. We—"

"They aren't our friends," Bud protested.

"No matter. All four of us are going to trail them. If they corner Bigfoot, maybe we can keep them

178

from killing him. Don't you two stir out of this camper until we get back. Wish us luck."

"Luck," Grammy and Bud chorused.

"Maybe I should go with them," Bud murmured.

"No! Ab-solutely, positively no!" Grammy exclaimed.

Secretly Bud was relieved. He really wasn't anxious to flounder around in the dark woods, knowing a wounded wild creature was somewhere roundabout.

Grammy unloaded her rifle and returned it to the closet. "There's nothing we can do until they return. Why don't you lower the table and fix the cushions so you can stretch out? I'm going to crawl back in my sack." She handed Bud a blanket from the closet shelf.

"I'm too jittery to sleep," Bud said. However, he was glad to wrap up in the blanket. The camper was chilly. He pressed himself into the corner and leaned his head back so he could keep watch out the window. As soon as his heart stopped pounding and he relaxed, he fell asleep. It was well past sunrise before he wakened. "Did you hear any shooting?"

Grammy had not.

"Good." Bud started biting his fingernails. Poor Bigfoot! Was he hiding somewhere, bleeding, in pain, unable to pry off the trap? "Bigfoot's strong enough to open that trap, I bet. But would he know enough to do it?"

There was no way of knowing, Grammy said. Actually, the more she thought about it, the more positive she was that they had heard a mountain lion screaming.

"I'll never, never forget those awful sounds." Suddenly Bud clenched his fists and pounded his head. "Oh, no! I was so upset I forgot to use my tape recorder!"

Grammy was terribly sorry she hadn't remembered it, too. To distract Bud, because he was becoming more and more upset, she asked if he wanted to make hotcakes for breakfast. He didn't. He would eat cereal and toast, and afterwards hike to the fallen cedar. "I've got to see for myself if the trap is gone."

Grammy said they would stay in camp until Mr. Eads returned.

"But he might be gone all day. If he starts taking pictures, he'll forget about us."

Nevertheless, Grammy stated firmly, she and Bud were not going into the woods.

Bud grumped all during breakfast. While he was dribbling honey on his fourth piece of toast, he had an idea. "Bigfoot needs help. Someone has to find him, and pry that trap off his leg. Why don't we hike to Joe's camp and tell him why he's got to show us where Bigfoot hides out." Also, Bud wanted Joe to know that neither of them had anything to do with the trap.

Again Grammy said they had to wait for Mr. Eads.

Fortunately the photographer and his companions did return shortly after. They were weary and frustrated. They had not found Bigfoot, nor footprints which could be identified positively as Bigfoot's. But the trap was missing from the hole, and the ground and shrubs roundabout were badly torn up. They had followed a bloodied trail almost to the top of the mountain without overtaking any wounded creature. However, they had caught up with Mr. Ward and Mr. Neilson when they stopped to rest. Jim Finch had pressed on alone in his grim hunt. Mr. Ward admitted Jim had set the trap. Now Mr. Neilson planned to return to camp, drive down the mountain and telephone for a hunter who had trained hunting dogs. He also was going to alert a man who used a helicopter for spotting elk for hunters in the fall. Mr. Eads ended by saying, "This place is swarming with Sunday-hunters. Frankly, I don't know what to do now."

Bud knew. He said they should climb to Joe's camp, and plead with the old Indian to guide them to Bigfoot's lair. "If men are going to hunt with dogs and a helicopter, we've got to move fast."

Eads queried Harry. "What do you think?"

"Whale of a good story," he answered.

Eads checked his watch. "We'll be ready to leave in a half hour."

When they all reached the logging landing, Mr. Eads parked the truck where it would not make problems for the loggers. Bud waved at several of the Indian crew, but they didn't wave back. Grammy said that was because they were concentrating on their dangerous work, and Bud shouldn't have distracted them.

"Okay, young fellow, lead the way up the mountain," Eads urged impatiently.

Bud was so intent on setting a good pace that a quarter hour passed before he realized his bits of red yarn were missing. "I know I left some along here." He pointed out the Indian blazes, so Harry could take notes and Eads could photograph them. After more climbing, Bud exclaimed, "Something's funny. I know I'm on the right trail but someone has removed my markers." His face darkened with suspicion. "Either Sam or Joe had to do it. They're the only ones who know this trail."

Maybe Sam walked down to the landing yesterday afternoon for supplies, and removed them then, Grammy guessed aloud.

"The loggers didn't tell us that," Bud argued.

"Maybe Sam arrived after they quit work. His father could have cached the supplies in the brush. You mustn't keep jumping to the wrong conclusions," Grammy said sharply. "Sam has a right to keep strangers from bothering his great-grandfather."

Mr. Eads fidgeted while they talked. "Who cares if your blazes are gone? Can you still lead us to Joe's camp?"

Bud could, and did. It was deserted. Although everyone shouted, neither Indian appeared. Their belongings were gone, too.

"Why would they leave?" Bud asked.

"Probably because they don't want to talk to us," Grammy guessed. Then she chuckled. "Or maybe my 'Indian' food made them sick."

Bud wailed, "Now we'll never know where to find Bigfoot and see if he needs help." He leaned against a tree, tears in his eyes. "He's probably bled to death by now, anyway."

Grammy gave Bud a brisk shake. "Now you listen to me, youngster. You don't know that was Bigfoot we heard last night. You don't know he was caught in a trap. You don't know that Joe could have shown us where Bigfoot hides out. The old boy might have been pulling your leg."

As much as he hated to, Bud had to admit his grandmother could be right.

Mr. Eads distracted Bud by asking him to pose, sitting under the Indian shelter.

"Do it," Grammy urged. "I bet neither Ronnie nor Doug ever sat in a genuine Indian shelter."

Bud not only complied; he posed gladly. Afterward he described Joe for Harry, and took the tape recorder from his knapsack so Harry could hear the old Indian chanting. Mr. Eads had Bud pose again with the tape recorder in hand, and pretend he was recording monster sounds. "We're going to have a feature article that will make headlines all over the country!" Then he suggested, "Let's divide up and search the mountaintop. If Joe led you to believe he could take you to Bigfoot's hiding place, then it can't be too far from here."

Everyone was agreeable. However, Harry said he had to be on his way out to Eureka by late afternoon. He would write the rough draft of the article while Jack and Phil developed the film, and put the whole feature together after he arrived home. It would have to be on the newspaper editor's desk before 10:00 A.M. if it was to be published in tomorrow's newspaper.

The search turned up nothing interesting. Bud set a fast pace down the mountain because he wanted to talk to the loggers before they quit work at 4:00 P.M. But even they could tell him nothing. "Or wouldn't," he guessed when he described the conversation to his friends. "They said they hadn't seen Sam or Joe, and didn't know where they were."

"They could be telling the truth," Grammy said.

"Well, somebody took my yarn markers," Bud insisted. "Who else would?"

He and the others walked on to watch logs being loaded on a truck. One of the loggers, rifle in hand, was patrolling the entrance to the landing. On the way out Mr. Eads asked why.

"Gotta keep those fool Sunday-hunters outa here," he answered irritably. "The whole mountain is crawlin' with 'em."

"D'you know if anyone caught Bigfoot?" Bud asked anxiously.

The man grunted. "Are you kiddin'?"

Scarcely a quarter mile down the road they encountered a raggle-taggle assortment of trucks, pickups, jalopies, cars, motorcycles, and bicycles. Men and boys armed with everything from rifles to sling shots were thrashing around in the timber, or gathered in small groups, talking. The ground was littered with beer bottles, plastic cups, and empty potato chip bags. The campground was even more crowded, a heavy pall of wood smoke and dust hovering over the open area. Here again people were running back and forth like ants.

The moment Eads parked his truck, some rushed over to ask, "Did you see Bigfoot? Did you hear anything?"

"Nothing," he answered, so emphatically that they withdrew. Harry disappeared into the camper to write while Eads, Jack, and Phil sought the portable darkroom. Grammy and Bud strolled to their camper. When they discovered someone had taken all their firewood, Bud was furious. Grammy was relieved that the strangers hadn't helped themselves to the table and stools. "What say we have a bath and rest?"

As tired and discouraged as he was, Bud wanted to meander around the campground and talk to people. Mr. Ward's campsite was deserted, but he spied Mrs. Neilson. Maybe her husband had returned. Grammy knew it was useless to argue. "All right, but don't you dare sneak off to the cedar tree."

Bud promised. First, he talked to Mrs. Neilson. Her husband and Mr. Ward were still out hunting. Someone Jim Finch knew had arrived with dogs. She heard that a helicopter had landed down the road, the pilot reporting he had spotted nothing out of the ordinary. That was all she knew.

Others lounging about told Bud nothing he didn't already know. None expected to see Bigfoot during the day. However, as soon as it was dark, they would patrol the road and be ready to shoot at anything that moved.

Bud scurried back to the camper. "I don't think we better go monster hunting tonight, unless Mr. Eads says it's all right."

The photographer emphatically advised them to stay in camp, and leave the camper outdoor lights on all night. "And you sleep inside," he advised Bud.

"What"ll we do tomorrow? Just sit around until all the people leave?" Bud asked worriedly.

Mr. Eads and Jack planned to leave early, when there was enough light so they wouldn't be mistaken for monsters, and return to Bluff Creek. "You two can come along, if you like, Wear tennis shoes. There are places where you have to wade the creek." He felt if they saw fresh footprints, it could mean the big-footed creature had not been caught in the trap.

"I sure hope we do find fresh tracks," Bud said fervently.

Grammy patted his shoulder. "So do I, before you worry yourself sick."

The next morning Bud and Grammy dressed, packed the knapsack, and waited inside until they saw Mr. Eads emerge. They put the portable table and stools in the camper for safekeeping, locked the windows and doors, and joined their friends.

"Where's Phil?" Bud whispered.

"Still in the sack. He's going to remain here to guard our property and yours."

Mr. Eads drove slowly up the road, passing the vehicles parked on the dirt shoulders. Fortunately none blocked the entry to the logging road which angled down toward the creek. He parked his truck, so it blocked the road, and locked it. Then the four hiked to the creek, where Eads said, "We'll follow upstream about two miles to where the creek forks. The boys and I checked the larger one yesterday, and we'll look at both today. They must trickle off into springs higher up because there's no lake sketched on the Ranger District map."

The search to the headwaters revealed no fresh tracks. However, Bud did see those from which Jack Eads had made the plaster casts for Bud and for his father. The deep impressions were dried out, the edges crumbling and less distinct. Still, no one would mistake them for bear tracks.

Grammy steadied Bud when he lifted his right foot to hold it above one of the giant prints. "Hold it!" Eads ordered. When Bud stiffened, the photographer laughed. "Relax. Don't smile so fiercely. Don't look at me, look at your feet!" After that Jack steadied Bud so Grammy could take a picture of him with her Polaroid. After the film developed, Bud gloated, "Wait'll the guys back home see this."

When they returned to the place where they had entered the creek, Mr. Eads said it was early enough to explore downstream a mile. Would they like to do that? Bud answered enthusiastically, "Yes!" If they saw fresh tracks, he might be willing to believe that Grammy was right about a mountain lion being caught in the trap, and not Bigfoot.

Again, he was disappointed. They saw no tracks at all. When Mr. Eads saw how upset he was, he took great pains to explain, "Look, over the years I have learned that Bigfoot prowls a small area for a short time, and then vanishes for six weeks or more. If he wasn't caught in the trap, all the noise and shooting and crowds could have frightened him off."

"But something got caught in the trap!" Bud cried.

No one tried to argue he was wrong.

It was almost supper time when they returned to the pickup and drove back to the campground. All were surprised to see most of the monster hunters were gone. This included Jim Finch's truck, the Neilson's rig, and the motorcyclists. They soon found out why. Jim and the hunter and dogs had returned with the carcass of a mountain lion. The men had pried the trap from its left hind leg after shooting it. Knowing well that they had broken the law by killing the big cat out of season, they all made a hasty departure. The Sunday-hunters also lost interest, and one by one drove down the mountain.

Bud looked as if a great burden had been lifted off his shoulders. "I'm sure sorry about the lion, but I'm so glad Bigfoot wasn't hurt."

Everyone agreed to that.

The strain of mountain climbing day after day, and the build-up of tensions had drained everyone's energies. Thus they cheered when Phil appeared in the doorway of the camper and shouted, "Come 'n' get it!" He had a hot meal ready for his famished companions.

While they were all eating, a motorcyclist turned off the road and braked to a stop by the camper door. When the man pushed back his helmet, Bud shouted, "That's Harry! Maybe he's brought the newspaper article."

Harry Elston had done that. As he spread the pages of the newspaper on the hastily cleared table, he told Bud, "You're going to be famous, son. The editor allowed a full page for photographs and didn't blue-pencil out a single word of the text." Then he stepped back so that Bud, Grammy, Mr. Eads, Phil, and Jack could gloat over seeing their pictures published alongside a fast-paced, exciting story.

Jack whooped. "Golly, Dad, I look like Bigfoot's son in this picture."

"Serves you right for not shaving."

Grammy clucked. "My land, I look a thousand years old. I should have tucked in my shirttail."

All Bud could say was, "Wow, wow, and double-double WOW!"

The feature article was so lengthy that Harry suggested they all sit down and let Bud read it out loud. "It's about him, mostly."

"Everybody ready?" Bud asked, his voice quavery with excitement. "Okay, here goes . . .

190

" 'Last Saturday an extraordinary young man from Boise, Idaho, reached remote Bluff Creek in the Six Rivers National Forest, fifty airline miles east of Eureka. His goal was to track down Bigfoot, the fearsome here-again, gone-again, man-ape monster that has lured thousands to the mountains of northern California. But this young man was a different kind of hunter. He had no gun, no trap. He was armed solely with a camera, his only bait pancakes which he cooked on his grandmother's griddle. His only desire was to prove Bigfoot was real, so thousands and thousands of other ecology-conscious young Americans would join him in a campaign to save this rare creature from destruction.' "

Bud's jaw dropped. He looked at Harry. "Is that what I did?"

Everybody laughed.

Bud read on and on. Finally the article concluded, " 'So young Bud Miller has joined the small fortunate group of Bigfoot believers who have actually seen the monster. True, he didn't get to walk up and shake hands with the creature. But, as we all know, nobody *meets* Bigfoot.' "

Bud leaned back, rolled his eyes, and wallowed in joy. "Grammy, I'm famous, I'm famous! Wait'll Ron and Doug see this. Wait'll Larry and Pam see it. They'll have to quit picking on me now. I'm no longer the Number Five Nobody in the Miller family."

"You never were the Number Five Nobody."

Bud didn't care whether he was or not.

He'd come to the mountain, had seen the monster, and was taking home a plaster cast of a monster footprint as proof. Deep down in his heart, secretly, cross-his-heart-and-never-tell, he was relieved he *hadn't* met Bigfoot face to face. Now he would have lots of time to make plans to save Bigfoot. Once he had a good plan, maybe he could come back and Joe would give him a hand. After all, it was high time Bigfoot learned to trust somebody. And why not— if that somebody's name just happened to be Bud Miller?